P9-ASJ-102

THE
BANDIT KINGS

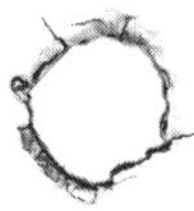

THE BANDIT KINGS

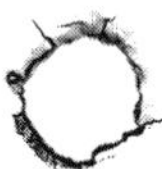

FROM JESSE JAMES TO PRETTY BOY FLOYD

ROGER A. BRUNS

CROWN PUBLISHERS, INC., NEW YORK

'The Cimarron Rose" by Grover Leonard, courtesy of the Oklahoma City Public Library.

"Pretty Boy Floyd" by Woody Guthrie, courtesy of the Guthrie Foundation.

Published by Crown Publishers, Inc., 201 East 50th Street, New York, New York 10022. Member of the Crown Publishing Group.
Random House, Inc. New York, Toronto, London, Sydney, Auckland
CROWN is a trademark of Crown Publishers, Inc.
Manufactured in the United States of America
Design by Kay Schuckhart
Library of Congress Cataloging-in-Publication Data
Bruns, Roger.
The bandit kings : from Jesse James to Pretty Boy Floyd / by Roger A. Bruns. —1st ed.
p. cm.
Includes index.
1. Outlaws—West (U.S.)—History. 2. Criminals—West (U.S.)—History. 3. West (U.S.)—History. 4. James, Jesse, 1847–1882. 5. Floyd, Pretty Boy, 1904–1934. I. Title.
F594.B88200 1995
978—dc20 94-37350
CIP

ISBN 0-517-59153-7
10 9 8 7 6 5 4 3 2 1
First Edition

CONTENTS

PROLOGUE

Jesse James.

(National Portrait Gallery, NPC. 88.206)

Charles A. "Pretty Boy" Floyd had a hero. One of the early twentieth century's most infamous bank robbers, Pretty Boy once declared to a newspaper reporter, "Jesse James was no punk hisself."

The great legends and folk stories of the western bandits, the tales of trains nabbed, guns notched, and banks nailed—it all passed from one generation to another. The days of Jesse and the Youngers, the Daltons, Butch and Sundance, those days of bank robber gangs on horseback, wielding Colts and Winchesters, gave way to the later days of Dillinger and the Barkers, Clyde Barrow and Bonnie Parker, Alvin Karpis, and Pretty Boy Floyd. No longer were the bandit kings riding horses; they were driv-ing Fords. But they still craved notoriety, still fired the imagination of the public, still tried to match the daring and bravura of bandit gangleaders past, still inspired writers, reporters, songwriters, and other legendmakers to turn their lives of crime and butchery into heroism.

hn Dillinger, 1934.

ional Archives, 306-NT-92280)

1

The Legacy of Bill Quantrill

The West in 1865 as depicted in *Harper's Weekly*. The Cosy Home Saloon in Virginia City, Nevada. (Library of Congress, LC-USZ62-61322)

It is of a fearless highwayman,
a story I will tell...
It was on the Nebraska prairies he
commenced his wild career,
and many a wealthy gentlemen
before him stood with fear.

QUANTRILL. NOW THERE WAS A NAME TO BOIL EMOTIONS. TALK TO A YANKEE AND YOU'D HEAR THAT QUANTRILL WAS A FIEND, A MANIACAL, MURDERIN' SON OF A BITCH; TALK TO A REB AND YOU'D HEAR JUST THE REVERSE—THAT HE WAS A patriot, a defiant hero defending right, honor, and justice.

Quantrill. The man almost defies characterization because legend has spilled over in exaggeration, contradiction, and bizarre twists. Bizarre, indeed. He died in 1867, and was buried in 1992—at least some of him was. It's true; it's all in the story. But Bill Quantrill's tale is part of a larger one—the story of the western outlaw gang, a story notched into the history of Civil War violence.

He always looked young, with that soft, blond, wavy hair; he was as slender, some said, as a woman. It was hard to believe that he'd killed a man back in Mendota, Illinois. Born in Canal Dover, Ohio, on July 31, 1837, Quantrill was the first child of Thomas and Caroline Quantrill. His father, a tinsmith and sometime schoolteacher, died in 1854, and Bill decided to follow his father's career in teaching. Bright and energetic, the youngster first taught in a country school

Violence, as the artist Thomas Benton asserted, was part of the "History of Missouri." His mural hangs in Missouri's statehouse in Jefferson City.

(Missouri State Museum)

near his home in Canal Dover and then in several other schools in Ohio, Indiana, and Illinois. In Mendota, he took a part-time job at a lumberyard; it was there, on the job, that he killed an intruder. At least self-defense had been his alibi. Although he was released from custody, many people in Mendota doubted the kid's word, thought he might be a cold-blooded murderer. They talked about his devious manner, the steely look in those eyes, the cool, calculating manner. Quantrill left town and headed farther west.

Rich land awaited in Kansas and Missouri, a couple of friends said, a chance for a quick stake and fast bucks for a man with ingenuity and guts. Quantrill reached Kansas

Territory in March 1857. He was nineteen years old but didn't look a day older than sixteen.

When Quantrill came to Kansas, he entered a volatile region already engrossed in the heated debate over extending slavery into new territories. Although it would be another four years until the Civil War would break out, here in Kansas pro-slavery and anti-slavery forces had already clashed.

In 1854 the delicate balance between the supporters and opponents of slavery had been violently shaken by the passage of the Kansas-Nebraska Act, Senator Stephen A. Douglas's attempt to ameliorate the growing controversy. The Illinois senator, positioning himself for a run at the presidency, attempted in the Kansas-Nebraska bill to implement in law the idea of "popular sovereignty"—the idea that residents of new territories should decide for themselves whether to allow the extension of slavery.

Although the idea of popular sovereignty seemed fair and democratic on the surface, many people, including Abraham Lincoln, a young lawyer from Springfield, Illinois, thought it dangerous. Opening up new areas to slavery, Lincoln reasoned, would provoke violent competition between the contending forces. Northern settlers, Lincoln said, wanted to have "a clean bed with no snakes in it."

Just as Lincoln feared, the competition between the two sides over the future of Kansas and surrounding areas turned the region into a bloody combat zone by the time Bill Quantrill arrived. Anti-slavery leaders in New England recruited new settlers to travel west. Southern pro-slavery leaders did the same. Rigged elections, lynch mobs, random killings, guerrilla violence—in Kansas the sectional hatred over slavery flared, foreshadowing the bloodbath that was to engulf the nation a few years later.

Abolitionist raiders, called "jayhawkers," conducted burning and pillaging raids from Kansas into the neighboring slave state of Missouri, especially in border communities near Kansas City. When pro-slavery raiders retaliated, many

William Quantrill in Confederate uniform.

(Kansas State Historical Society)

were killed by Union forces. The Confederate guerrillas then "took to the brush," as they said, and were soon dubbed "bushwhackers." Thus, a whole generation of tough, teenage boys on the Kansas-Missouri border grew up brandishing guns and knives and anticipating armed conflict at any moment.

Quantrill befriended a few abolitionists in Kansas when he first arrived, and even accompanied the "red legs," as some of the jayhawker guerrillas called themselves, on forays into Missouri to steal slaves and livestock. But his relationship with the abolitionists quickly soured. Quantrill soon began to travel in the company of their enemies. By the summer of 1858 he roamed the state with bushwhackers and then traveled farther west, working as a teamster, prospecting for gold, stealing horses, rustling cattle, running with an assortment of gamblers and gunslingers, charging from one violent escapade to another. When Quantrill spent time in the northeastern section of Indian Territory, he was fascinated with the guerrilla combat techniques used by the Cherokees. Quantrill's gentle face, his soft blond hair, and his fastidious demeanor camouflaged an ever-growing, intensely fierce obsession with military techniques and a cavalier attitude toward violence.

In an act of brazen defiance, Quantrill decided to move to the abolitionist stronghold of Lawrence, Kansas. Here, in a city founded by abolitionist politicians and populated by abolitionist gunslingers, Quantrill engaged in a clandestine enterprise to capture and return livestock and fugitive slaves previously stolen from Missouri farmers by abolitionists. Here in the rabid center of abolitionist power and intrigue, Quantrill, using the pseudonym "Charley Hart," made daring border runs, outwitting and mocking his pursuers. His hatred toward Kansas and abolitionists grew more intense and more fanatical. He resolved to punish them both.

When Quantrill was apprehended in late 1860 and charged with robbery, arson, and slavecatching, he quickly escaped and plotted revenge. On a cold December day in 1860 in Osawatomie, Kansas, four jayhawker abolitionists set off to Jackson County, Missouri, to free the slaves of a well-to-do farmer named Morgan Walker. But one of the four men, slightly built, blond-haired, was not hunting slaves; he was hunting abolitionists. When the four reached the Walker home, an ambush party, arranged by Quantrill, waited. At the signal from Quantrill, a blast of gunfire swept through the bodies of the three unsuspecting abolitionists. According to one account, one of the men survived the shotguns but did not survive a revolver blast through the mouth delivered by Quantrill himself.

A few days after the incident in Jackson County, on December 20, 1860, a state convention in South Carolina declared "that the union now subsisting between South Carolina and the other States, under the name of the 'United States of America' is hereby dissolved." By February 1861, six more states had followed. The *South Carolina Mercury* proclaimed, "The revolution of 1860 has been initiated."

With the outbreak of the war, the hostilities between pro-slavery, pro-Confederate Missourians and anti-slavery, pro-Unionist Kansans degenerated further. Gangs of Kansas jayhawkers plundered and set afire towns and farms in Missouri; bushwhacker guerrilla bands from Missouri retaliated.

At the head of the most celebrated of the guerrilla gangs rode Bill Quantrill, his marauding and terrorizing skills now finely honed, his taste for new exploits growing. Some said that the young, fair-haired man even giggled when things got especially tense.

Ambushing Federal patrols and then disappearing, harassing pro-Unionist settlers, burning and stealing, Quantrill's band, a few friends at first, began to acquire new recruits eager for mayhem. They had been freed by the war from the shackles of regular, ordered life. With Quantrill they could roam the countryside playing out dark fantasies with impunity, could even imagine that the violence was for some grand cause. Here with Quantrill, they could, for the supposed glory of the Confederacy, kill, terrorize, and steal. For many young roustabouts, the war was liberating.

On March 7, 1862, Quantrill's band assaulted the small town of Aubry, Kansas, pillaging stores, shooting indiscriminately, killing several citizens. Union troops stalked the guerrillas across Jackson County, cornering them on a couple of occasions only to be outmaneuvered.

Like many of the gang leaders to come, like Jesse and

Bloody Bill Anderson, one of William Quantrill's lieutenants and one of Jesse James's mentors.

(State Historical Society of Missouri, Columbia)

Pretty Boy and Dillinger, Quantrill was exceptionally intelligent, quick-thinking, brash and confident, totally convinced of his invincibility, willing to play cunning fox to the dull-witted dogs on the hunt. Bring on all the jackass Federals and abolitionist clowns in Missouri! Well armed with shotguns and Colt revolvers, dodging from one skirmish to another, finding allies among the local populace who shielded them in barns and fields and fed them not only food but information, the Quantrill bushwhackers flourished.

On August 11, Quantrill's raiders helped regular Confederate troops overtake a Federal garrison in Independence, Missouri. The operation earned the guerrilla leader a captain's commission as a "partisan ranger." Officially recognized as head of "Confederate Cavalry Scouts," a title bestowed by a Confederate commander, Quantrill now became an employee of the Confederate government. Now even more emboldened, he spurred the guerrillas on to new conquests in Missouri and Kansas. At Olathe, they killed a dozen men; at Shawneetown another twenty, mostly civilians. An observer at Shawneetown talked of the horror of seeing men shot down "like so many dogs." Near Independence, the raiders ambushed and killed Missouri militiamen. At Westport they murdered nearly two dozen Kansas cavalrymen. A Union man in Kansas called Quantrill "a monster of the worst kind." Another said, "As long as Missouri and Kansas have a name and a history, they will remember with shuddering and bitterness the name of Quantrill."

Bill Anderson rode with Quantrill. His family moved to Kansas from Missouri in 1857; father, mother, three boys, three girls. The Council Grove area offered rolling prairies and relative quiet and serenity for the farmer and family. But the war changed all that. Of Southern background, the Andersons refused to join loyal Yankee forces when the war began. In May 1862 a judge accused the elder Anderson of horse stealing. In a bloody gunfight a few days later, Bill Anderson's father was killed. The young Anderson left town, rounded up several Yankee-haters, and returned to see the judge. Council Grove, Kansas, thus became the site of gruesome vengeance. The judge, along with his brother-in-law, was shot, thrown in a cellar, and buried beneath the building above, which was then torched.

During the war, the area around Council Grove became a haven for Southern sympathizers and gained the reputation of being a "rebel town." Bill Anderson helped make his father's town safe for bushwhackers. Later, Anderson led a group of raiders through eastern Kansas, burning houses and shooting local Federal sympathizers. But once again, the Anderson family suffered. In the summer of 1863, a squad of soldiers captured Anderson's mother and sisters and escorted them to a makeshift prison in Kansas City. Within two weeks, the old, poorly constructed prison building collapsed, crushing one sister to death and permanently injuring another. Bill Anderson burned for more revenge. They would soon call him "Bloody Bill."

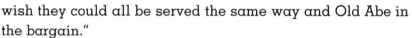

Stories arose, gruesome stories, of Bill's scalping Union soldiers and tying the scalps on his horse's bridle. And many Union enemies cheered him on. One Confederate woman from Missouri wrote to her brother, "I thought for a while he acted brutal but now nothing he does can be too bad with me. I now laugh when I see the scalps of the Feds tied to the bridle bits, and wish they could all be served the same way and Old Abe in the bargain."

Cole Younger also rode with Quantrill. Cole's father, Colonel Henry Younger of Harrisonville, Missouri, was for several years a county magistrate and served a few terms in the state legislature at Jefferson City. The wealthy Colonel Younger owned much land and many slaves. He was proud of his Southern heritage. But faced with war's choice, Colonel Younger remained loyal to the Union. In late 1861, however, some Yankee jayhawkers swaggered into Harrisonville and unceremoniously made off with many of Younger's possessions, including some forty horses. The prominent Missourian, insulted to the core, switched sides. His allegiance now lay, he announced, with the Confederacy.

The following June, returning home from a trip to Kansas City, Colonel Younger met a cadre of Union militia. They left

"A Guerrilla Raid in the West," a *Harper's Weekly*'s Thomas Nast depiction of a Quantrill raid "so that our readers may understand the sort of war the rebels are waging."

(Library of Congress, LC-USZ62-31174)

him dead on the road, shot in the back. Yankees later burned down his mansion.

Retaliation. In August 1863, Cole Younger led fifty guerrillas to Pleasant Hill, Missouri, home of many Northern loyalists, a town whose name would suddenly turn darkly ironic. Cole Younger and his men turned much of Pleasant Hill into ashes.

Frank James also rode with Quantrill. In the 1840s a Baptist missionary named Robert James and his wife, Zerelda, settled in Clay County, Missouri, near the small town of

Pencil sketch of Quantrill's raid on Lawrence by Colonel S. Enderton.

(Kansas State Historical Society)

Kearney. There, the couple built a log cabin and cleared nearby land for a farm. On January 10, 1843, they celebrated the birth of a son and named him Alexander Franklin James. As years went by, the first name didn't seem quite right with family and friends; everyone began to call him Frank. In 1847 a second child arrived, another boy, whom they named Jesse Woodson James. In Jesse's case, the first name worked out just fine.

Robert James read the stories in local papers and heard from travelers passing through of gold strikes in California, of hard-luck sodbusters suddenly made wealthy. He headed west with the same dreams held by thousands who had gone before and who would go later. He never returned, dying of pneumonia in the California gold fields. Zerelda married again but later divorced. Her third marriage was to a doctor named Reuben Samuels.

Close to the James farm, only a few miles down the dirt

road to Lee's Summit, lived four brothers who had left home and settled on their own. Their name was Younger—Coleman, James, John, and Robert. The James boys and the Youngers cavorted together through their teenage years. The advent of the war turned mischief into something more deadly. Frank James and Cole Younger joined up with a man named Quantrill. Later, Jesse would ride off with one of Quantrill's lieutenants, a man with the nickname of "Bloody Bill."

From the early days of the war, the pro-slavery guerrillas had talked about a grand attack on the town of Lawrence. Think of the psychological triumph of pillaging the pit of abolitionism; the home of Charles Robinson, leader of the anti-slavery political forces in the region; the home of Jim Lane, one of the North's most despicable hell-raisers; the home of John Speer, one of abolitionism's most obnoxious newspaper publishers. Think of the alarm that would fill newspaper columns in the eastern papers; think of the glory in the slave states when word spread of this victory.

On August 10, 1863, Quantrill revealed to his fellow guerrillas a plan to sack Lawrence. Some of the men hesitated. But several days later, when word arrived that the prison in Kansas City housing members of Bill Anderson's family had collapsed and killed one of his sisters, the bushwhackers agreed it must have been a Yankee plot. All doubts about whether to attempt the dangerous attack on Lawrence were swept away in angry promises to punish and avenge.

Dawn. August 21, 1863. William Quantrill and a huge force of approximately 450 guerrillas including Cole Younger and Frank James charge into Lawrence, carbines and Colt .36-caliber revolvers blazing. They kill men; they spare women and children. For four hours the raiders destroy the town; they burn and maim in a wild frenzy of violence, all the while screaming obscenities. The townspeople, taken totally by surprise, are dumbfounded by the horror.

Newspaper publisher John Speer loses two sons, John Junior, shot down at the corner of Jentry and New Hampshire, and Robert, burned to death in the offices of his father's paper.

George Collamore, mayor of Lawrence, awakens to the sounds of several of Quantrill's men entering his home. Collamore and a friend who was staying with the family hide in a well beneath the house. Here, they suffocate as the raiders burn the house.

There were scores of stories that hideous morning in Lawrence—of heroic attempts to save friends; of luck that led to life or death; of three thousand people trying to fend off the savage, long-haired riders invading their town.

And what of Quantrill? For a while during the slaughter, he drove around the streets in a buggy, laughing. Later he ascended the steep heights of Mount Oread to look down on the scene below. He saw the business district in ruins; he saw houses across the town in flames; he saw bodies of men lying in the streets. At least 150 men died that morning, the most devastating guerrilla or cavalry raid of the Civil War. One eyewitness said, "The town is a complete ruin . . . everything of value was taken along by the fiends . . . I cannot describe the horror."

Union pursuit of the raiders ended in such frustration and failure that Brigadier General Thomas Ewing, Jr., signed an extraordinary order in late August. Residents of the county of Jackson and two adjoining western Missouri counties were to be evacuated. The guerrillas' civilian allies who had been sheltering and feeding them would be removed, thus cleansing the region so that the marauders would have less chance to survive.

Although thousands of residents were displaced by the order, although homes and farms and buildings were torched and sacked by Union forces, Quantrill and the others avoided capture. In October 1863, near a Federal fortification in Baxter Springs, Kansas, they confronted a column of Yankee cavalry and a wagon train led by Major General James Blunt. Whooping and hollering, many dressed in Federal blue as disguise, the Confederate guerrillas wiped out the Yankee column in a few minutes. Only Blunt's swift horse saved him from the fate of most of his party. Nearly one hundred men lay dead; some of the bodies were stripped and mutilated.

Quantrill was soon swilling captured whiskey, toasting the power of the greatest bushwhacker band ever assembled. To strike suddenly and with force; to overwhelm not only physically but also psychologically; to employ wit and cunning to offset an opponent's numerical strength; to use civilian allies (gained from actual friendship or, most often, from intimidation and terror) for information and supplies; to be unpredictable; to be proficient and skillful with all the tools of the business, especially firearms—these were the lessons Quantrill passed on to his men: Cole Younger and Frank James and Bill Anderson and the others. These were the lessons they passed on to Jesse.

Years later, law enforcement officials in Washington and marshals in Oklahoma lamented the difficulties they were having in trying to understand Pretty Boy Floyd's movements, those unpredictable, evasive maneuvers, his lightning strikes and disappearances in the Cookson Hills where it seemed every citizen was a possible accessory to his escapes. Floyd and John Dillinger and the others of the later generation also learned the lessons well.

Quantrill's star seemed to fade after Baxter Springs. For a time the guerrillas were in the Cherokee Nation killing Indians. Chief John Ross and other Cherokee leaders wrote that the raiders were indiscriminately murdering Indian farmers and burning their villages—almost, it seemed, for sport.

As Quantrill headed farther south into Texas, he was urged by Thomas C. Reynolds, the Missouri Confederate governor-in-exile, to join the regular Southern military. Reynolds told Quantrill that commanders of headstrong guerrilla forces usually wound up with personnel problems, that mutiny and power struggles inevitably plagued such outfits, and that the commander usually ended up dead or disgraced.

But Quantrill's precipitous fall from power came sooner than even Reynolds expected. Some of the guerrilla leader's men left the band after charging Quantrill with an unequal division of money taken in some of the raids. A few other raiders seemed genuinely shocked by the ruthlessness of some of their own comrades and, probably fearing that their own fates might be the same as that of the slaughtered men in Lawrence and Baxter Springs, decided to get out.

One of Quantrill's lieutenants, George Todd, a man of almost singular psychopathic viciousness, even dared to face Quantrill down early in 1864. Placing a gun to Quantrill's head, Todd asked the guerrilla leader whether he was scared of him. Quantrill could only say yes, he was afraid of him. This act, played out in front of a number of the men, seemed almost unthinkable in its audacity, given Quantrill's own reputation for brutality. But then George Todd, like Quantrill, played by no known code or rules. Todd that day compromised Quantrill's bravado and his image of fearlessness. Quantrill and his teenage mistress left the gang and went into hiding for several months in northern Missouri, letting the war go on without them.

Bloody Bill Anderson didn't take leave of the fighting. And Bill and Frank James added a new recruit. Jesse James was a tough kid who had watched Union militia beat his stepfather and humiliate his pregnant mother. Some of the Union soldiers had whipped Jesse himself. He was now part of the gang, raiding, ambushing, killing. In September 1864, at Centralia, Missouri, fifteen miles from Columbia, the band of about thirty men terrorized the community, set fires, robbed a stage entering the town, robbed and beat passengers from an incoming train, and slaughtered twenty-five unarmed Union soldiers on furlough. A few days later, they wiped out nearly 150 Union militia and mutilated the corpses. Frank James later credited his brother with killing the militia commander, Major A. V. E. Johnson. For Jesse, as it was for so many teenagers caught up in the war, there were few restraints. For Missouri Confederates, killing a militiaman was a patriotic thing, and in Bill Anderson's bunch, butchery was encouraged.

In October 1864 it all ended for Bloody Bill. He was killed in a fight outside Richmond, Missouri. The dead guerrilla leader, clad in an embroidered shirt, still clutching his Colt revolver, was beheaded. For the Union soldiers, it seemed the appropriate thing to do. A few days earlier, at a small battle near Independence, many of Quantrill's remaining guerrillas, including George Todd, had perished along with some regular Confederate troops. In Missouri, as in most parts of the United States, the grand cause of the Confederacy now seemed certainly a lost cause.

Quantrill now decided to take to the guerrilla road again. Recruiting several of the remaining raiders still in Missouri, including Frank James, Quantrill raided small-town stores and picked his way through Arkansas and Tennessee into Kentucky. But the force never grew to more than fifty men.

In Kentucky the Federals sent Captain Edwin Terrill, a turncoat Confederate, to track down the gang and its leader, who was now going by the name of "Captain Clarke." In May 1865, near Bloomfield, Kentucky, in Spencer County, Quantrill was disabled by a bullet that hit him in the back and paralyzed his legs. He died in a Louisville hospital several weeks later, on the same day that the citizens of Missouri ratified a new state constitution abolishing slavery. He was a mere twenty-seven years old.

Bill Quantrill was buried in Kentucky, but, just as in life, he seemed to keep moving; he simply refused to molder. In 1887 Quantrill's mother decided she wanted her son back in Ohio. Along with one of Quantrill's boyhood friends, Bill Scott, she disinterred the skeleton and took it to Canal Dover for burial. Showing some of the nonchalance and ingenuity displayed by Quantrill himself, Scott decided on an entrepreneurial venture. He kept his old friend's skull and several leg and arm bones in the hope that some collectors might be interested in bidding for them. Scott was never able to amass a great profit from the enterprise. But the skull found its way into the Dover Historical Society and the bones to the museum of the Kansas State Historical Society in Topeka.

The town of Last Chance Gulch at the end of the Civil War. Later, it would be called Helena.

(Montana Historical Society)

* * * * * * *

OCTOBER 24, 1992. HIGGINSVILLE, MISSOURI. CONFEDERATE MEMORIAL STATE PARK. Over 127 years after Quantrill's death, some of him is buried again. With a backdrop of musket fire and smoke, with full military honors and a Roman Catholic ceremony, a hank of hair and several bones are borne in a small wooden casket to the graveyard where rows on rows of Confederate markers display fluttering Rebel flags. Robert Hawkins III of Jefferson City delivers the eulogy to an audience of Civil War buffs dressed in gray uniforms and packed in the cemetery chapel. "He belongs here," declares Mr.

Hawkins, "here with those who were truly his people. Here in a chapel where men worshipped who revered his memory as the unrepentant resistance to military occupation of this state which was brutally harsh in all its respects." A descendant of one of Quantrill's raiders, who acted as one of the pallbearers, declares, "He did what he had to do."

Regrettably, Hawkins and the others were not completely satisfied with the day's events. The Dover Historical Society, which had the skull in its possession, had not cooperated by turning it over. The society's chairman, Les Williams, said later, "I think they are going overboard in Missouri, with two hundred people and a big ceremony over a hank of hair and five bones. I think all the bones should be buried in one place and the largest part of the Quantrill bones are here."

Williams was wrong, at least in one respect. Actually, more than three hundred people had gathered for the event in Missouri. But apparently Williams was right on another matter; most of the Confederate guerrilla's remains—the ones that Bill Scott had not taken for commercial gain—were, indeed, in Dover's Fourth Street Cemetery.

And so the war goes on. Bill Quantrill can still, nearly a century and a half later, boil emotions. And whatever his influence on events of the Civil War, one thing is unmistakable—he and his lieutenants trained a group of bandit outlaws whose influence spanned generations.

In the folk song about Quantrill that survived the Civil War, the Confederate hero myth lives, a "bold, gay, and daring" outlaw, a Robin Hood from the mountains who descended with his band to the prairies to rob the rich and divide it "with widows in distress." In the history of western bandit outlaws, the Robin Hood hero myth emerges over and over again. Cole Younger, Jesse James, Pretty Boy Floyd, and others all became subjects of western folktales and folk ballads.

As for Quantrill, his life and exploits even spawned a professional society that lives to protect his image from historians and others who would distort and disgrace it. Mr. Kimberly Colwell, president of the William Clarke Quantrill Society of Wichita, Kansas, recently said, "William Clarke Quantrill was no scoundrel. Partisan soldiers greatly aided the Confederate cause, and Quantrill excelled in his role. To many, he was, and is, a hero." Mr. Colwell referred to a letter written by an ex-Confederate soldier who was nursed to health by Quantrill and his men. To the soldier, as well as to Mr. Colwell and his society members, and to the three hundred who attended the burial in Higginsville, Quantrill was a loyal Confederate, brave, faithful to the cause. And besides, said the soldier, "Around here it was always considered a better idea to be his friend."

Oh, Quantrill's a fighter, a bold-hearted boy,
A brave man or woman he'd never annoy.
He'd take from the wealthy and give to the poor
For brave men there's never a bolt to his door.

2

THE JESSE LEGEND

The face of the young Jesse James.

(National Archives, 208-PR-10X-2)

PRIL 3, 1882; ST. JOSEPH, MISSOURI.** Jesse James dies.

APRIL 22, 1882; NEW YORK CITY. *The Judge*, a satirical magazine in its first year of publication, proposes that a monument be built in Jesse's honor. While depicting train and stage robberies, the monument would also feature a model of Jesse's home. Inside the house, amidst guns, daggers, and revolvers, would be three plaques bearing the following messages: "Bless Our Home," "What Is a Home Without a Revolver," and "What a Friend I Have in Jesus and My Revolver."

LATE SUMMER, 1882; SPRINGFIELD, MISSOURI. A blind woman stands in front of the courthouse singing an ode to Jesse, a song composed by a man named Billy Gashade shortly after Jesse's death. Passersby drop coins in the blind woman's tin can.

NOVEMBER 1883; TOOTLE'S OPERA HOUSE, ST. JOSEPH, MISSOURI. A troupe of actors performs a drama about Jesse James. The company features a special attraction on-stage—two horses that purportedly belonged to the infamous outlaw. One horse, Roan Charger, has been identified by a local man as having been in Jesse's stable, only yards from the room where the outlaw was gunned down by Bob Ford. The other horse, Bay Raider, although lacking similar eyewitness testimony to sub-

From a fading photograph more than a century old, Frank and Jesse display their long-barreled revolvers.

(The Denver Public Library, Western History Department)

stantiate claims to equine immortality, had been, nevertheless, one of Jesse's horses, according to stage company spokesmen.

1900; KEARNEY, MISSOURI. Jesse James's mother continues to decorate her son's grave at the homestead with flowers, some of which have bloomed from seeds sent to her by well-wishers from across the country. She still entertains visitors (for a tourist fee) with tales of her outlaw sons. She has per-

Jesse and Frank James soliciting funds aboard a train.

(State Historical Society of Missouri, Columbia)

fected the performance to include tears of grief and promises of revenge against the Pinkertons and other enemies. An extra twenty-five cents will get the visitor a few pebbles from Jesse's grave.

MARCH 1903; MINNEAPOLIS, MINNESOTA. A bone from Jim Younger's jaw, shattered at a bank robbery in Northfield, Minnesota, in 1881, is placed on display at the Minnesota State Historical Society. It is a relic of the state's most celebrated gun battle.

1903; COLUMBIA, MISSOURI. Frank James and Cole Younger, survivors of the James-Younger gang, have formed the James-Younger Wild West Show, an extravaganza that, along with gunfights and horse stunts, re-creates a stagecoach robbery. On August 27, 1903, the show visits Columbia and the local newspaper declares: "Their crimes can not be excused, but they can be forgotten, now that they have been pardoned under the law, and can and should be covered with that Christian charity which hides a multitude of sins."

October 1927; Kearney, Missouri. Local townspeople, debating whether to erect a monument to Jesse James in his hometown, ignite a national debate over the issue of this special outlaw's place in history. Why glorify a crook? In the *New York Times,* writer Eunice Fuller Barnard laments the possible loss of her own favorite villain, Jesse. A monument would amount to the bestowal of respectability on a true superbandit: "It is almost a tragedy," says Eunice Barnard, "this snatching from childhood of one of its few clandestine joys. It is like a nightmare in which father, taking the Jesse James thriller from under one's pillow, nods approvingly . . . it is like forcing Peter Pan to grow up and go to the office every day at nine o'clock."

July 2, 1931; in the mountains near Wetmore, Colorado. A man named James Sears, who has lived as a recluse for many years, dies. Shortly thereafter, a friend of Sears, a man named William White, reveals that the old loner had admitted to him that he was actually Jesse James, that the supposed killing of Jesse a half century before had been a hoax perpetrated by the outlaw to escape punishment, and that the dead man in the ground in St. Joseph, Missouri, was more than likely a member of the James gang who had died of typhoid fever.

April 21, 1932; Excelsior Springs, Missouri. Local citizens and Jesse James experts investigate the claims of another man who insists he is Jesse. "No, he isn't," shouts Frank Milburn, who, as a young shoemaker, had made boots for the outlaw. "Jesse James wore six-and-a-half boots. This fellow couldn't get his foot in one." Mrs. Jesse James, Jr., wife of the outlaw's son, who is in Missouri as an expert witness, produces one of Jesse's boots for the test. It doesn't fit.

April 1933; Nashville, Tennessee. Mrs. Mary James Barr, daughter of Jesse James, returns to her birthplace. This wood frame homestead perched on a knoll had, decades earlier, given

Cole and Jim Younger, Missouri Rebels.

(State Historical Society of Missouri, Columbia)

her fugitive father a mile's view in all directions. Mrs. Barr tells reporters that her father had been misunderstood, that his legendary foul deeds had been exaggerated and fabricated. "He was accused of many more things than he ever did," she says. "He could not have been with the Younger brothers when they robbed the bank at Northfield, Minnesota, because he was right here at the time."

1948, LAWTON, OKLAHOMA. Two reporters for the *Lawton Constitution,* Frank Hall and Lindsey Whitten, write a story giving credence to another purported Jesse. One J. Frank Dalton, a man almost as aged as Jesse would have been had he lived, has claimed to be the famous outlaw himself. The story suggests that the man who moved to St. Joseph, Missouri, in November 1881, a "Mr. Howard," was not Jesse but a man named Charley Bigelow. The story suggests that Jesse sang in the choir at his own funeral. It suggests that Jesse later graduated, with honors and under an assumed name, from the University of Michigan.

APRIL 4, 1972; KEARNEY, MISSOURI. Fannie Shanks, a restaurant owner and promoter of a forthcoming Jesse James festival, explains to a reporter why she and other residents of the town are preparing to honor a criminal. "The James episode is part of history now," Fannie says. "Why not celebrate it with some square dances and shooting contests and the like?" For Mina Spicer, longtime owner of the Kearney Variety Store, the whole Jesse business is a bit weird: "Back in my day he was an outlaw. It was never talked about. For your kids growing up today it's history. They don't think of him as a bad guy. We did." Good guy or bad, Jesse will be honored by this day's festivities; the county will restore his home. The forty-acre farm where Jesse was born has been placed on the National Register of Historic Places.

1980; ACROSS THE UNITED STATES AND ABROAD. United Artists releases *The Long Riders,* a film on the James gang, directed

The James house, Kearney, Missouri.

(Library of Congress, LC-USZ62-22986)

by Walter Hill. The film has a mountainous gimmick—the outlaw brothers are played by movie actor brothers. The James brothers are played by the Keach brothers; the Younger brothers are played by the Carradine brothers; the Miller brothers are played by the Quaid brothers. Even the assassin brothers are played by actor brothers—Christopher and Nicholas Guest are Charlie and Bob Ford.

MAY 24, 1981; LIBERTY, MISSOURI, TEN MILES NORTHEAST OF KEARNEY. Town officials place an inscribed bronze plaque on a two-story brick building. The inscription says that the building is the site of the first daylight bank holdup in United States history and that the robbery was pulled off by the James gang. It makes little difference to townspeople here in Liberty that historians have now almost unanimously agreed that the robbery that occurred here in 1866, leaving a dying bystander and a bank deficit of over $60,000, was certainly not perpetrated by Jesse. Liberty's citizens want part of the legend. "Here is where America's greatest folklore history began and ended," says Milton Perry, Clay County superintendent of historical sites. "He's to this county what Robin Hood is to England."

* * * * * * *

Ninety years after his death, Jesse still makes a name for himself in Clay County, still brings out the crowds. Most of the people who had any dealings with the James family are long since gone. Grover Albright, nearly ninety, a former postman, remembers Jesse's brother, Frank James, in his last days. "Frank was one heck of a guy whenever I had any dealings with him," says Grover.

The James house, northeast of Kearney, is still open for tourists; inside is the bed in which the brothers were born and a picture of Jesse taken shortly before his death. Under the direction of a University of Missouri archaeologist, the outlaw's casket was moved from its former gravesite closer to the house. Other renovations of the farm have made it an even more inviting place for tourists. Richard Weber, a local real estate agent and president of the Kearney Chamber of Commerce, believes that Jesse can make Clay County even more than it is today. "You can go anywhere and people have heard of Jesse James," he says. Mr. Weber says that the latest Jesse James festival will include a carnival, a parade, and the popular mock bank robbery, with tourists substituting for the James gang, toting guns with blanks and moneybags filled with bubble gum. Just trying to get a little closer to the legend.

The story itself has been told, retold, and embellished; subjected to psychological and analytical interpretation; set to music; made into novels, short stories, television and radio presentations, ballads, and art; researched; and elevated to myth and legend. Jesse James has become as much a part of American letters and culture as other folk heroes from Daniel Boone to Charles Lindbergh.

In post–Civil War America thousands of men and boys stayed on the road, inured to lives of fighting and surviving on the run, most permanently displaced from homes and families, many without jobs, some suffering from alcoholism and other assorted physical and emotional maladies. Some hit the freights looking for work; others wandered on horseback, looking for a stake, a quick fortune, a new start. Many headed west into Kansas, Oklahoma, and Wyoming and farther on.

The frontier, with its scattered population and lures for quick fortunes and power, with its relative lack of public order, tempted all sorts of personal and social deeds and misdeeds. In the wide-open cattle towns and mining camps, in the new settlements from the Dakotas to California, towns just given names, just now making identities, some folks looked to turn their lives around. For many, the near anarchy of the war had seemed intoxicating, and their best friendships now were with former war buddies. They loved the violence, the flirtations with death, the abandon. In the unsettled, raw towns of the frontier and prairie they could, perhaps, make something happen.

Shortly after the war, some Confederate bushwhackers, still not whipped by the Yankees, continued to carry on what they saw as the grand cause. Ex-guerrilla fighters rode into old abolitionist towns like Abilene and Dodge City and raised all kinds of hell. When the citizens brought in professional pistoleers to wipe out the rowdies, they usually called for ex-Yankee soldiers such as Wild Bill Hickok, Wyatt Earp, and Bat Masterson. In Missouri, especially, the ex-Confederate boys held forth. They warred on banks and railroads, most owned by Northerners, and many Southern sympathizers among the citizenry cheered them on.

Jesse and Frank James, and many other ex-Confederate soldiers and guerrilla fighters in Missouri and neighboring states, had no desire after the war to settle down on their farms to a tedious life and meager existence under the control of Yankees. For them, the war had meant power and exhilarating uncertainty and chance. Under Quantrill and Anderson they had rampaged and pillaged with relative impunity; they had made others the victims in their glorious day and were not about to take on that sniveling role for themselves. They would still be guerrillas after the war, would still use the small gang hit-and-run attacks they had learned from their mentors, would continue their own war, make the raider life a profession, make names for themselves, make money, and never surrender.

On a bitterly cold February day in 1866 the Clay County Savings Association in Liberty, Missouri, was robbed by a gang of about a dozen ex-Confederate raiders from Jackson and Clay counties dressed in Union Army blue coats and other items of Union apparel. Over $60,000 in currency, government bonds, gold, and silver were stolen. After the confusion and panic and wild shooting during the robbery, a bystander, a student at William Jewell College, lay dead in the street. The local paper in Liberty declared, "The murderers and robbers are believed . . . to be . . . old bushwhacker desperadoes" who should be "swung up in the most summary manner." In the next few years, banks in Lexington, Savannah, and Richmond, Missouri, and in Russellville, Kentucky, were similarly robbed.

Although Jesse and Frank James had, during the war, ridden with some of the men accused in the press of several robberies, and although later dime novelists, historians, and balladeers have placed the James boys at one or more of these banks, local authorities and vigilantes at the time were not on the trail of the James brothers. They were, nevertheless, on the trail of some of their friends. And some of the Missourians were ready to act out the sentiments delivered by the Liberty newspaper.

Two nights after the Richmond, Missouri, robbery, a rough encounter in which the mayor of the town was gunned down, a mob broke into the Richmond jail and hung a suspect named Felix Bradley, a horse thief who might have had nothing to do with the robbery. In a jail at Warrensburg, southeast of Richmond, a former Quantrill raider named Thomas Little, also suspected of involvement in the Richmond robbery, was given a mock trial and executed on the spot. Soon, two other ex-Quantrill guerrillas were hunted down by vigilante mobs and murdered. And, in March 1868, back in Richmond, two more ex-raiders held as robbery suspects were busted out of their cells and hung from nearby trees. The Richmond, Missouri, jail was rapidly becoming one of the most unsafe spots in America.

On December 7, 1869, two men entered the Davies County Savings Bank in Gallatin, Missouri. One of the men calmly shot the cashier, a former Union militiaman, through the head and heart and then wounded another bank employee. During the bandits' escape, one of their horses became excited in the melee and raced away, temporarily dragging its rider. After disentangling himself from the stirrup, the bandit crawled onto the other horse and the two highwaymen managed to leave town relatively unscathed. Later, townspeople identified the agitated horse as one belonging to the Jameses. As a posse approached the James-Samuels farm in Kearney, Jesse and Frank escaped on fresh horses. The James brothers were now linked to robbery and murder.

A newspaper report in the *Kansas City Times* anticipated trouble ahead for the law: "They know every foot-path and by-road . . . they are cool, determined, desperate men, well mounted and well armed." That day in Gallatin marked the beginning of years of headlines, of many posses, of escalating rewards, and of tall tales; it marked the beginning of a robbery career unsurpassed in its audacity, unparalleled in its longevity.

The career flowers: June 1871, Ocobock Brothers Bank, Corydon, Iowa; April 1872, Deposit Bank, Columbia, Kentucky; September 1872, the Kansas City Fair, Kansas City, Missouri. In Kansas City, the gang struck at midday in the midst of several thousand fairgoers and robbed the fairgrounds ticket office. In the *Kansas City Times,* journalist Major John Newman Edwards, a former Confederate adjutant under General Joseph O. Shelby and a man who through the years became the James gang's most ardent defender and promoter, saw in this kind of attack the stuff of heroic daring. Like Arthur and his Round Table knights, like Lancelot winning over Guinevere, like Ivanhoe, lance raised, like the most chivalrous figures ever imagined by the bards, declared Edwards, the James gang was riding into western outlaw history. "With them," Edwards waxed, "booty is but the second thought; the wild drama of the adventure first. These men never go upon the highway in lonesome places to plunder the pilgrim. That they leave to the ignoble pack of jackals." No, the James brothers rode in daylight, in open display, witnessed by the admiring multitudes. John Edwards churned out this prose after the boys in one of their daring escapades had accidentally shot a small girl in the leg. Edwards never changed his mind about Jesse; his frequent articles about the bandit, justifying his outlawry in the name of Southern justice and Robin Hood valor, helped turn Jesse into a modern exemplar of medieval heroism.

In July 1873, the James gang extended its repertoire from banks to trains. Train robbing was not a Jesse and Frank invention (the Reno gang of Indiana garnered credit for that in the late 1860s), but the boys added their own signature to the art. At a curve on the Chicago, Rock Island, and Pacific near Adair, Iowa, the gang loosened a rail, attached a heavy cord to its end, and waited. When the train approached they pulled the rail, forcing the engine into the cinders and onto its side, crushing the engineer. The gang members collected money from the express company safe and valuables from the passengers, and, shouting Rebel yells, rode off.

At Gads Hill, Missouri, on the Iron Mountain Railroad about a hundred miles south of St. Louis, the gang plundered another train after taking control of the depot; and near Hot Springs, Arkansas, they robbed a stagecoach. The newspapers were now revealing the names: Jesse and Frank James; Cole, James, John, and Bob Younger. Some reporters, taking their lead from John Newman Edwards, portrayed these men as ambivalent criminals driven to their deeds by wartime antagonisms, as social and class protesters, as symbols of masculine defiance stirred by codes of honor. The papers told the story of Cole's returning money to an ex-Confederate soldier after a robbery, of Cole's declaring to another victim that Northerners had driven the boys into crime, and of Jesse's checking the hands of possible victims for calluses. Only individuals with soft or manicured hands were robbed, they said.

Some of the stories were rooted in single incidents; others were fabricated; all were kneaded and massaged beyond recognition. Fueled by these excited newspaper reports, by lurid articles in the *Police Gazette* and other magazines, by dime novels sold in drugstores and train stations, by tales growing taller with each retelling, the James gang, with each new exploit, gained more national attention.

Between 1870 and 1876, the James and Younger brothers and their cohorts carried their work into Kansas, Kentucky, Iowa, and Texas. As sheriffs and marshals across the West had no luck trapping or even tracking the gang, with embarrassment piling on embarrassment, bank, express, and train company officials decided to call in the Pinkertons, the hired guns, the "Pinks."

* * * * * * *

The motto: "We Never Sleep." The logo: a picture of an open eye surrounded by the words "Pinkerton's National Detective Agency." Founded by a son of an impoverished Glasgow weaver and sometime policeman, the private crime agency, named after Abraham Lincoln's confidant, Allan Pinkerton, had, from its earliest days before the Civil War, brought in scores of wrongdoers: burglars, forgers, embezzlers, diamond heisters, pickpockets, horserace scam artists, safecrackers, fences, rogues of all kinds and stripes. Railroads and banks across the country gladly paid premium costs to protect their interests. The Adams Express Company, for example, hired the Pinkertons to track down the Reno brothers, who had hit their baggage cars in several

Allan Pinkerton and his Civil War secret service.

(National Archives, 90-CM-385)

raids between Indianapolis and New Albany, Indiana. The Pinkertons were smart and relentless. During the war, Allan, his two sons, Robert and William, and their other agents had done intelligence and protection work for the Union forces. By the 1870s the Pinkertons' crime-solving doggedness and precision had gained international renown.

When Pinkerton agents took up the hunt for the James gang, they confronted even more difficulties than local law enforcement officials had faced. They were seen by much of the population as opportunistic hirelings of railroads and banks and other corporations, institutions viewed with hostility by much of the western public. They were outsiders, venturing into unfamiliar terrain amidst many people unsympathetic to their meddling. They had little personal knowledge of the habits, appearance, and tactics of the gang. But they were veteran professionals dedicated to upholding the reputation of the firm. As William Pinkerton

Allan Pinkerton, 1862.

(National Portrait Gallery, NPC. 78.276)

once said, "I do not know the meaning of failure."

The early efforts of the Pinkertons to corral the James gang were ignominious and tragic. One agent, attempting infiltration, tried to hire on at the James farm as an itinerant worker in March 1874 and was soon found with bullets through his heart and head alongside a road near Independence, Missouri. Shortly after the Pinkertons lost this agent, they lost two more in a shootout with the Younger brothers near Osceola. The Youngers also suffered a loss—brother John. Cole later wrote, "Poor John. He has been hunted down and shot like a wild beast, and never was a boy more innocent."

On a frigid night in late January 1875 the Pinkertons attempted to capture the James brothers at the Clay County farm. A posse of Pinkerton agents and local lawmen surrounded the darkened house, where they assumed the boys were spending the night. Posse members shouted for Jesse and Frank to surrender. No response. In an effort to fire the house and force the occupants outside, the men lobbed through the windows several Roman candle tubes filled with cotton saturated with turpentine. One of the posse members then threw in a seven-inch incendiary device. Dr. and Mrs. Samuels were inside with an eight-year-old boy, Archie, a half brother of Frank and Jesse. When the flaming iron ball crashed through the window, the Samuelses shoved it into the fireplace. It exploded. When the posse rushed in, they found the walls splattered with blood, the boy grievously wounded, and Jesse's mother bleeding from a serious wound to one arm. Mrs. Samuels lost her forearm; young Archie lost his life.

The events of those few minutes of botched law enforcement insured that the Jesse legend would grow to even more immense proportions. A hero craves public sympathy. The publicity resulting from the bungled attack gave the outlaw more than he could have ever imagined.

John Edwards, to no one's surprise, was outraged: "Men of Missouri, you who fought under Anderson, Quantrill . . . and the balance of the borderers and guerrillas . . . give up these scoundrels [Pinkertons] to the Henry Rifle and Colt's revolver." Although other reporters did not care to revive incendiary sentiments from the Civil War over the incident, they did pour out sympathetic columns to Jesse and his family. The *New York Times:* "Everyone condemns the barbarous method used by the detectives"; the *Chicago Times:* the fireball slaughter of former bushwhackers by so-called lawmen was merely an extension of Civil War hatreds that must be tamed; the *St. Louis Dispatch:* all former guerrilla fighters who had turned to crime in desperation after the war must be allowed amnesty for their crimes committed during the war and the full protection of the law for crimes committed after it; the *Kansas City Times:* the lawmen had employed "common 'thief catchers' who outrage farmhouses, carry off peaceable citizens, kill . . . boys, blow off the arms of women . . ."

Press indignation was mirrored early on among some members of the Missouri state legislature who, following the

The logo and motto of the world's oldest private detective agency.

(Reprinted with permission from Pinkerton Security & Investigative Services; Pinkerton's Inc., Encino, CA 91436)

lead of the *St. Louis Dispatch,* introduced a bill providing for the pardoning of all ex-bushwhackers for their wartime deeds. But before the legislature acted on the measure, the James gang was apparently involved in the murder of a neighbor suspected of aiding and abetting the Pinkertons. With public opinion about the gang oscillating wildly, legislators rejected the bill. The public, the press, the politicians—all shared confusion and mixed sympathies and disgust about the gang, shared a bizarre concoction of local pride, wartime animosities, fear, and fascination.

The Pinkertons, proud masters of detective craft, seemed to lose heart for the James gang manhunt after the farmhouse episode. The agency quietly faded from the scene. Robert Pinkerton later called Jesse "the worst man, without exception, in America. He is utterly devoid of fear, and has no more compunction about cold-blooded murder than he has about eating his breakfast."

By late summer 1876, the James gang was at its zenith of power, pulling off brash daytime hits with impunity in Missouri. Cocky, seemingly invincible, the boys decided to take their act north. One of the gang members, William Stiles (alias Bill Chadwell), persuaded Jesse and the others that his home state of Minnesota would be a rich hunting ground of vulnerable banks. Decked out in long linen dusters, they rode into Northfield, Minnesota, on the morning of September 7, 1876—Jesse and Frank James; Cole, Bob, and Jim Younger; Chadwell; and two other gang members, Clell Miller, former guerrilla under Bloody Bill Anderson, and Charlie Pitts, a friend of Cole Younger from Jackson County.

Three men entered Northfield's First National Bank while two stood guard outside and three waited farther down the road. Cole later remembered "a crowd of citizens about the corner, also our boys sitting there on some boxes. I remarked

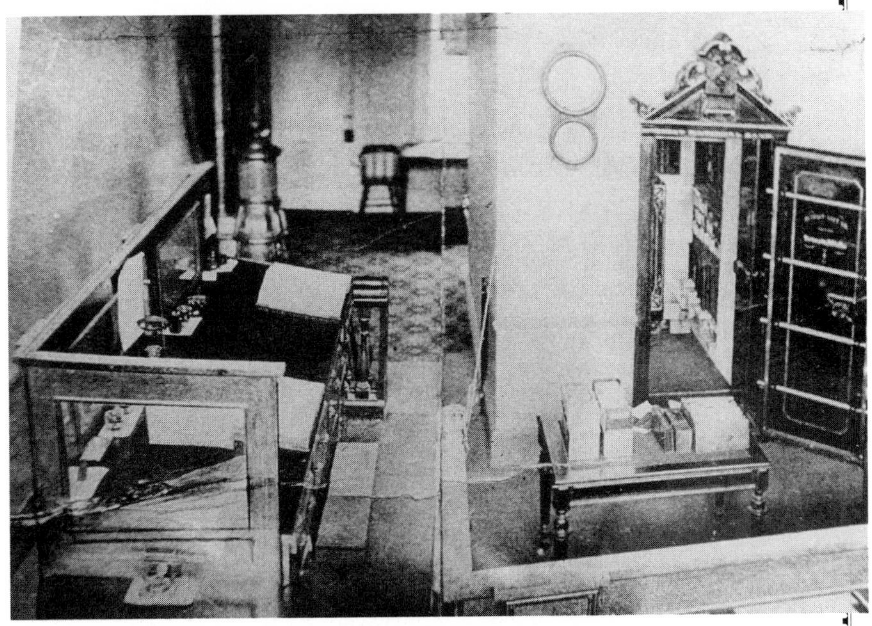

Interior of the First National Bank of Northfield, Minnesota, 1876.

(Northfield Historical Society)

Exterior of the First National Bank of Northfield, Minnesota, 1876.

(Northfield Historical Society)

to Miller about the crowd and said 'Surely the boys will not go into the bank with so many people about.'" The men did go in. Younger told Miller, who had confidently lit up a pipe, to put it out. All hell was about to explode.

When the cashier refused to open the safe, one of the outlaws slit his throat and shot him. A bank teller ran from the building, suffering a shoulder wound. Several citizens of Northfield, now aware that a robbery was in progress, quickly grabbed rifles, pistols, and shotguns and turned them on the men outside the bank. Chadwell and Miller crumpled dead from their horses. As the three outlaws in the bank raced outside, they managed to kill the local sheriff and a Norwegian immigrant who was in the way, mounted horses, and charged down the main street, which had quickly turned into a war zone. Bob Younger's elbow was turned into bloody shreds by a rifle blast, and his horse went down after being shot. Bob was picked up by one of his brothers. The Younger and James brothers managed to get out of Northfield, but the Younger brothers were all seriously wounded. Things had not gone well for the vaunted gang; this was not precision bank robbing.

As the telegraph carried word throughout Minnesota that the James gang was on the run and in trouble, as farmers and townspeople turned out by the hundreds to organize the most elaborate manhunt ever seen in the state, the gang, drenched by unrelenting rains, unfamiliar with the countryside, suffering from critical wounds, wandered in circles in the Minnesota wilderness. After several days of trailing the injured men, the posse overtook Charlie Pitts and the three Youngers in a swamp near Madelia, Minnesota. In a weak exchange of gunfire, Pitts fell dead, and the Youngers, ripped with bullet holes, their clothes red and shredded, surrendered to the posse.

Bob Younger, at the time of the trial for the holdup of the First National Bank of Northfield, Minnesota, September 7, 1876.

(National Archives, 111-SC-93373)

Jesse and Frank, who had separated from the others, escaped. Miraculously, the Youngers managed to survive their massive injuries and began life sentences in the Minnesota State Penitentiary at Stillwater. Bob Younger, quoting Cole, told a reporter, "We tried a desperate game and lost. But we are rough men used to rough ways and we will abide

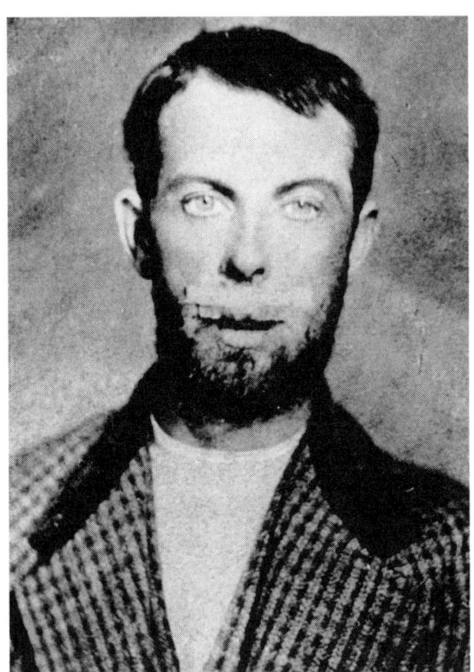

Jim Younger, recovering from a gunshot wound to the face, at the trial for the Northfield, Minnesota, robbery attempt.

(National Archives, 111-SC-93375)

by the consequence." Cole, also interviewed by reporters, expressed regret for his crimes, talked of his boyhood joy of attending Sunday school, quoted from the Scriptures, and wiped tears from his eyes. Some of his listeners were impressed. The man had suffered eleven bullet wounds at Northfield and at the skirmish in the swamp and had survived. Cole would carry those eleven bullets in his body for the rest of his life.

After Northfield, the James brothers disappeared. Enemies and admirers vied to shed light on their movements and intentions. Some said they went to Mexico; others insisted they headed west. Both were now married and had children; perhaps they had settled down to an honest, Christian life. Frank later said that they had moved their families around to large cities such as St. Louis and Nashville. Police and private detective agencies still had only vague descriptions of the outlaws—tall, bearded, lean, and so forth—descriptions that, in the West of the 1870s, fit more than a few men.

On October 8, 1879, the gang was back in business. With the Youngers now in forced retirement, the James brothers took on new partners, some petty robbers and horse thieves. They hit the Chicago and Alton line for $6,000 near the

Glendale Station in Jackson County, Missouri. Townspeople later talked about a note left by the gang: "We are the boys who are hard to handle, and we will make it hot for the boys who try to take us."

O JESSE WAS A MAN AND FRIEND TO THE POOR
HE WOULD NEVER SEE A MAN SUFFER PAIN,
BUT WITH HIS BROTHER FRANK, HE ROBBED THE CHICAGO BANK,
AND HE STOPPED THE GLENDALE TRAIN.

On July 15, 1881, at Winston, Missouri, in Daviess County, the boys hit the Chicago, Rock Island, and Pacific, killing the conductor, a passenger, and viciously beating several other individuals.

Cole Younger at the time of his trial in 1876.

(National Archives, 111-SC-93338)

On September 7, 1881, on the fifth anniversary of the Northfield raid, the gang robbed a Chicago and Alton train at Blue Cut, east of Independence, Missouri, by laying a pile of rocks and logs on the track. The outlaws beat the express car messenger with pistol butts. The train's engineer later testified that the bandit leader, during the robbery, shook his hand and gave him two silver dollars "for you to drink the health of Jesse James." Just a little more nourishment for the legend.

It was now clear to almost everyone, except the most jaded Jesse James apologists, that the bandit was not still in business to avenge the South. The latest raids had nothing to do with the old bushwhacking days, nothing to do with punishing ex-Yankees or embarrasing bank and railroad interests because they were owned by Northerners, nothing to do with social banditry or antiestablishment statements or robbing the rich to somehow benefit the poor. At a trial of a James gang member in Jackson County, Missouri, an old Confederate stronghold, several witnesses, for the first time, revealed Jesse James's complicity in robberies. The prosecutor later said that the trial convinced many people in Missouri who had been afraid to talk about the gang that it was now possible to offer valuable information and still live.

Charlie Ford, accomplice with his brother in the assassination of Jesse James.

(National Archives, 111-SC-93371)

In July 1881, Thomas T. Crittenden, governor of Missouri, met with railroad and express company officials in St. Louis. The purpose of the meeting: to raise a large amount of money for rewards to be paid for the apprehension of the James gang. In press reports around the country, editorialists had talked about Missouri, the sovereign state of crime; Missouri, the lair of bushwhackers and bank robbers; Missouri, the "State of banditry." Crittenden wanted the jibes ended. If state funds were limited, perhaps company coffers could be tapped. The railroad executives, also very tired of the James brothers, enthusiastically agreed to Crittenden's requests. "Rise en masse," implored Crittenden to the citizens of Missouri, "by day or night, until the entire band is either captured or exterminated." Bring in the brothers and receive $5,000 a head; another $5,000 each for their conviction; $5,000 more for the arrest and conviction of other participants in James gang crimes.

The reward offers lured the Fords, Bob and Charlie, two new recruits in the James gang. Charlie had been along on a September 1881 hit of the Chicago and Alton, and Bob was supposedly to see his first gang action in a robbery scheduled for April 4 at a bank in Platte City. The Fords, indeed, lusted for money—but not in the way Jesse had in mind; the Fords had decided to cash in on Jesse himself.

Bob Ford, the killer of Jesse, poses with his gun.
(National Archives, 111-SC-93370)

On April 3, 1882, at a house in St. Joseph, Missouri, where Jesse, under the alias of Howard, had lived for a time with his wife and two children, Bob and Charlie shared dinner with the outlaw and talked about the next day's plans. Jesse apparently remarked that the Platte City robbery would be his last and that he planned to take his family to Nebraska and retire on a farm.

But the Fords had been in personal contact with Governor Crittenden, who had given them assurances that the reward money was indeed there for the taking. In the living room of the James house, when Jesse for a moment turned his back to the brothers, Bob Ford drew a Smith & Wesson .45 and shot the infamous outlaw through the back of the head.

It was on a Saturday night, Jesse was at home,
Talking to his family brave,
Robert Ford came along like a thief in the night
And laid Jesse James in his grave.

Jesse had a wife to mourn for his life,
The children, they were brave,
But that dirty little coward that shot Mister Howard,
Has laid Jesse James in his grave.

Assassination by traitors, by plotters! What better way for a historical folk hero to perish! Major John Edwards, legend builder and glorifier of the saint, unleashed his untamed, soaring metaphors and analogies to do their work once again. Jesse James, said John Edwards, was like Julius Caesar. Or like another victim of assassination: "Indignation . . . is . . . thundering over the land that if a single one of the miserable assassins had either manhood, conscience, or courage, he would go, as another Judas, and hang himself."

Editorialists railed against the blood bargain struck by the governor of a state and cold-blooded killers. The unseemly plot darkened the history of Missouri, many said, even more than the black outlaw deeds of Jesse. Some refused to believe that Jesse had died. Rumors and wild tales of devious plots and escape and a new life for the bandit would continue to color the Jesse legend. A man like this could not possibly have been shot in the back, could not . . .

(For legends, for folk heroes, this kind of survival in the face of all evidence is not unusual, not in America, not in other countries. After Alexander I of Russia died, rumors persisted for many years afterward that he had not died at all, that a log had been laid in his coffin and that he had escaped to live as a monk in Siberia.)

Tried in St. Joseph on murder charges, Bob and Charlie Ford pleaded guilty, were sentenced to death, and were then pardoned by Governor Crittenden. Bob Ford later suffered the same fate as Jesse, shot to death ten years later in Creede, Colorado. His brother Charlie committed suicide a few years later.

Frank James surrendered to Crittenden at Jefferson City on October 5, 1882. On two separate occasions, once at Gallatin, Missouri, and later at Muscle Shoals, Alabama, he stood trial. Each time, sympathetic juries, lacking hard eyewitness evidence, voted for his acquittal. The James brothers, with years of bank, stage, and train robberies attached to their reputations, were never convicted of a single crime. Frank James, old, tired of the crime game, turned to other pursuits. He sold shoes, got a job as a theater guard, and then worked as a horserace starter. He raised Poland China hogs and Plymouth Rock chickens. For a time, he accepted speaking engagements to lecture on the theme "Crime Doesn't Pay"—all the while, of course, still trying to make it pay.

In July 1901, Cole and Jim Younger received paroles and left the Minnesota state prison. (Bob Younger had died of tuberculosis in prison in 1889.) Under provisions of their conditional releases, the men were not given full legal rights and were confined to the Minnesota borders. Jim and Cole soon found jobs selling monuments for the Peterson Granite Company. Jim, who had lost most of his jaw from wounds suffered at Northfield, fell in love with a writer named Alice Miller. Under terms of the parole, the ex-outlaw was not allowed to marry. Despondent, ill, Jim Younger, in October 1902, ended his life with a shot through his head in a shabby hotel room in St. Paul.

Mourners surround the casket of Jesse James—a stereograph by A. Hughes. (Library of Congress, LC-USZ62-50810)

The James boys and the Younger brothers now had one survivor each. Cole Younger and Frank James, boyhood allies, reunited for a time in their later days. They formed their own Wild West show, a kind of western circus popularized by Buffalo Bill Cody. Financed by a Chicago brewer, Cole's and Frank's show included "Russian Cossocks, Bedouin Arabs, American Cowboys, Roosevelt Rough Riders, Indians, Cubans, Western Girls, Mexicans, Broncos, Overland Stage Coach, Emigrant Train, The Siege of Deadwood and the World's Mounted Warriors."

Frank understood his status in national mythology and even tried to rationalize the career of the James gang in terms of the country's changing economic and political cli-

mate. "If there is ever another war in this country," Frank declared, "it will be between capital and labor, I mean between greed and manhood, and I'm as ready to march now in defense of American manhood as I was when a boy in defense of the South." The old Confederate avenger had become a budding Socialist.

Frank died in Missouri in 1915; Cole died a year later. But it was not Frank James or Cole Younger who were immortalized; it was not the men who served time or got old or took undignified jobs. It was Jesse, lean and daring, the outlaw who was not caught, the avenger of Southern rights, the fighter of the rich and their corporations, the Robin Hood.

Bob, Jim, and Cole Younger with sister Henrietta, September 1889.

(National Archives, 111-SC-93340)

A story handed down: When Jesse and his gang were in western Missouri shortly after the war, they had just robbed a local bank and were tired and hungry. They stopped at a farmhouse for some food. A young widow answered Jesse's knock on the door and invited the boys in for dinner. It turned out her

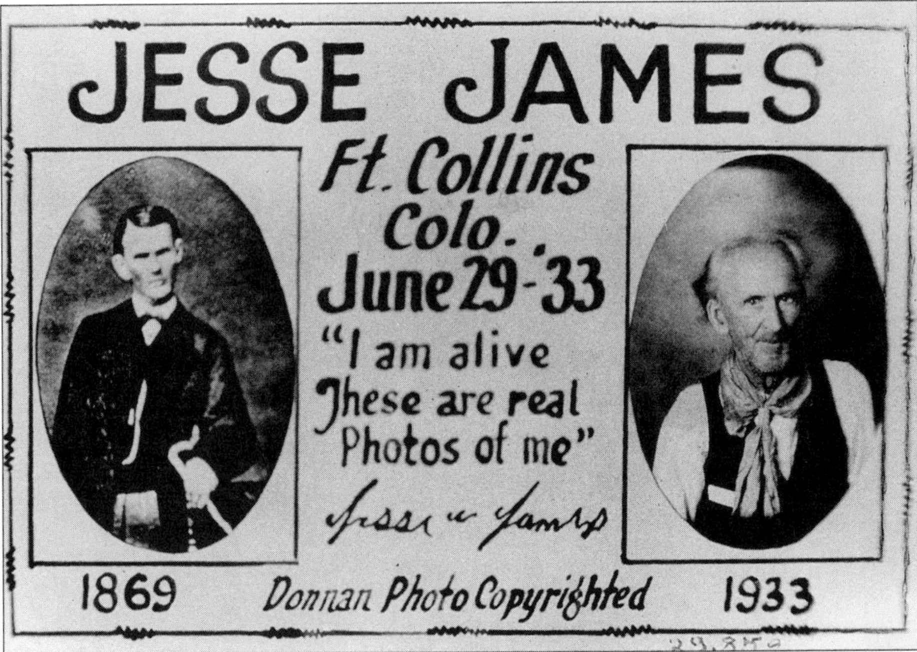

A number of men in the twentieth century claimed to be Jesse James. Some, such as this gentleman, made public stage appearances.

(Arizona Historical Society/Tucson, Portraits, Jesse James)

husband had been a Confederate soldier. The widow shared what food she had and Jesse handed her some money in return. But he noticed tears in her eyes. It seems that a banker was coming that very afternoon to foreclose on her farm. She had no money and Jesse was touched. He gave her several thousand dollars to pay off the entire mortgage. The woman was overcome with joy. After a couple of hours, a pompous banker showed up ready to take over the property. The widow handed him the money and sent him on his way. As he headed down the road toward town, an armed man jumped in front of his horse and stole the money. Yes, it was Jesse!

Years later the same story circulated in Oklahoma. It had to do with Pretty Boy Floyd. Woody Guthrie used it in a song.

3

THE BASS WAR

The law in Texas. Judge Roy Bean's building in Langtry was both a courthouse and a saloon. Here, one got ice, beer, and, sometimes, justice.

(National Archives, 111-SC-93343)

SEPTEMBER 18, 1877, 10:48 P.M.; BIG SPRINGS, NEBRASKA, A WATER STOP ON THE UNION PACIFIC LINE. Highlighted by a prominent moon, six riders arrive at the small station, destroy the telegraph equipment, abduct the stationmaster, and force him to red-lantern the Union Pacific eastbound express train Number 4. As the train rolls to a crawl nearing the station, the six men scramble aboard, four into the locomotive to overpower the crew, the other two into the express car to smash open the heavy boxes containing a gold coin shipment from the San Francisco mint. After beating the express messenger on the head and face with pistols to persuade him to open the safe, the two men in the express car hack at the boxes with axes and the loot spills over the car floor. Filling large bags with coins and bills, the two then march through the passenger cars forcibly collecting reluctant contributions.

After splitting the take, the six men head out in different directions. Two of the men trade for fresh horses and a nearly broken down buggy, hide the gold on the buggy floor, and head west, disguised as dirt-poor homesteaders from Kansas in search of a stake farther on. Stopped by soldiers, the two are asked whether they had seen men on horseback carrying Winchesters. The sol-

Sam Bass with fellow gang members J immie Murphy and Sebe Barnes. (National Archives, 111-SC-93366)

diers ride on. The two fake sodbusters continue their slow ride home.

❋ ❋ ❋ ❋ ❋ ❋ ❋

Visit Big Springs, Nebraska, over a century later and see a marker erected by state officials honoring one of the most famous train robberies in American history, a robbery that netted the bandits more than $60,000 in twenty-dollar pieces, a robbery that made an outlaw hero out of a man named Sam Bass. The inscription calls Sam "legendary"; in dedicating the marker, the state officials talked about his exploits and later demise—Sam Bass, train robber extraordinaire, bandit king, legendary successor to Jesse James, a man who created a war in Texas; Sam Bass, heroic, misunderstood, a man eulogized in song. Most of it was bunk.

He was born in southwestern Indiana, near Bedford, in July 1851, the son of farmers, Daniel and Elizabeth Bass. When he was ten years old his mother died; his father passed away three years later. Sam and his several brothers and sisters moved in with a maternal uncle named David Sheeks. It was soon clear why the uncle wanted the children—he wanted laborers. After working on the farm for a number of years, Sam ran away in 1870 and headed south, finally taking a job as a millhand in Rosedale, Mississippi. He had never been entered in a public school and could barely sign his name. He was now without family, without an education, and without money. He did manage to save some of his earnings in Mississippi and decided to travel farther west, dreaming about horses and cowboys and about making a name and a living.

Sam Bass was born in Indiana it was his native home
And at the age of seventeen, young Sam began to roam.

Dark, handsome, with a beard sweeping over his collar, he arrived in Texas in 1870. He hired on as a cowpuncher on the Carruth Ranch, about fourteen miles from Denton, a farming and livestock area. He became a crack shot and tough cowboy. Later, he worked at a hotel in town and as a roustabout for Sheriff Bill "Dad" Eagan. He acquired a reputation as honest and trustworthy. In 1874 he bought a racehorse and, after winning several local races, decided to take to the road for better competition. He traveled into Indian territory, southwestern Texas, and into Mexico, winning some races, getting a bit heady, and gambling most of his winnings away. He had tasted success, had made some money, and the taste was intoxicating. He wanted more.

HE FIRST WENT DOWN TO TEXAS, A COWBOY BOLD TO BE
A KINDER HEARTED FELLOW, YOU'D SCARCELY EVER SEE.

In San Antonio, Bass met Joel Collins, ex-bartender and cowboy. The older Collins mesmerized him with stories of making big money, easy money. The two became partners. At first, the business was legitimate, running steers from Texas to Dodge City, Kansas. But in 1876 Collins persuaded Bass to head farther north, into the Black Hills. There, the business became crime.

Their first effort, an attempt to rob the Deadwood stage, ended ignominiously. They killed the stage guard and got almost nothing. They kept at it but seemed always to pick stages that carried passengers with little cash—or, in one case, a stage that carried no passengers. But the two persevered. And Bass, as did other outlaws who gained big reputations, developed a trademark—he left each of the victims at least one dollar. Unfortunately for Bass and Collins, that amount in some cases almost equalled what the passengers were carrying.

With their inept start, the fledgling outlaw duo decided to expand. They recruited four veteran outlaws from Nebraska Territory—Bill Heffridge, Jack Davis, Jim Berry, and Tom Nixon. The group decided that stage robbery, the profession that had plagued Collins and Bass with such middling fortune, was not the answer. Their future was in trains.

This group of six masked men hit the Union Pacific at Big Springs. Bass and Jack Davis escaped in the buggy. Joel

Collins was not so fortunate. Along with Heffridge, he was killed by a posse near Buffalo Station shortly after the robbery. Berry was killed in Missouri. Nixon, holding most of Berry's money, disappeared. Even the determined efforts of the Pinkertons to locate the fugitive for several years failed. Tom Nixon had made his mark and his money, so he retired.

The Union Pacific heist was the richest in the annals of American train robbery up to that time, $60,000 in gold coins from the express shipment as well as money and jewelry from the passengers. Bass had established his reputation. The stage robber who had experienced such woeful luck in the past had now bagged a train more lucrative than any nabbed by Jesse or any other outlaw.

Bass went back to Texas in 1878 and rebuilt the gang with several of his old friends. The story in Denton was that Sam had struck gold big in the Black Hills and had traded in the dust for coins. His friends, however, were closer to the truth—Sam had struck it big in train lucre and was confident there was more there for the taking.

For some reason, Sam decided to warm up the new troops by taking on stages again, a dubious proposition given his former record as a highwayman. On December 21, 1877, the bandits stopped a stage near Fort Worth. Sam had picked another loser; two passengers handed over $43. A month later, they struck again, this time netting about $400, still a comparative pittance considering the contents of those boxes from the San Francisco mint. Once again, Sam gave up the stages for trains.

In January 1878 the gang hit the Houston and Texas Central and later the Texas Pacific. Sam's return to the tracks did not bring back the magic. In the first robbery the gang collected over $1,000 but was outwitted by an express messenger who successfully concealed a large amount of money in the stove of the car. Although the gang's other efforts were equally disappointing, Texas newspapers warmed to the tale of the Robin Hood outlaw who always gave back a buck.

With stories in the press stirring interest in Bass and his

escapades, tensions escalated among federal marshals, sheriffs, and private company detectives—and among bank officials and stage and railroad company executives. They all recognized a folk hero in the making; they all feared that the bad luck that had plagued the bandit in Texas would change as it had at Big Springs, Nebraska, and that the public would become his ally. The nefarious Bass was now only a slight menace; they needed to stop him before he became a serious economic liability and a threat to public order.

Governor R. B. Hubbard called in the Rangers. Major John Jones, Frontier Battalion, took charge. His slouch hat merging into a prominent mustache, the smallish major teamed with a Dallas peace official named Junius Peake to recruit a special company to prosecute what came to be known as "The Bass War."

Sam Bass was suddenly on a sure path to bandit fame. He responded magnificently, becoming as elusive as Jesse. All the newspaper hype, the rewards, the talk of bringing down and exterminating and hanging, the challenge of the Texas Rangers—it all seemed to fire the competitive juices. He led his buddies into the bluffs near Denton that he had known for years. Amidst the tangled thickets and swampy marshes and limestone cliffs, Bass maneuvered his comrades around and through and ahead of his pursuers. He knew intimately the timber-rich, rugged terrain where drop-offs could suddenly appear in front of a rider, where rattlesnakes thrived and multiplied, where, as one city reporter who had briefly traveled into the hills said, it wasn't daylight until midday.

Occasionally Bass and the other gang members would dart into communities for supplies; often they would lead posses and sheriffs and detectives through confusing mazes of paths known only by the local residents. A reporter from Dallas talked of hordes of professional gunmen and amateur bounty seekers and lawmen streaming into the woods in search of Bass and the promised rewards. The manhunt, he said, was almost comical: "They . . . fill the woods with little posses armed with pot metal shot guns and mounted on

Sam Bass? Some historians say yes; others say no. Several history books have included this photograph as a portrait of Bass, yet the resemblance to other authenticated Bass portraits seems slight.

(Prints and Photograph Collection, The Center for American History, The University of Texas at Austin)

spavined ponies to go chasing up and down the Cross Timbers shooting at one another, that there never was a chance to lead Bass into a trap." Sam Bass, in the early months, was winning the war.

Sam was also winning the image war. He now passed out twenty-dollar gold pieces to folks in the backwoods, ate dinners with them, succeeded, as did many successful outlaws, in making the community his shield. But avoiding capture was not enough; a bandit hero must successfully make great strikes. He planned new ventures. To hell with stages and trains; they were too uncertain. Some carried money; but most carried too little of it. On to banks! On to banks, where Jesse had made the great hits, where the Bass gang could justify in deed all the attention now being lavished upon it by the media and by law enforcement agencies.

On April 29, 1878, one of the Ranger companies got close. With the gang on one side of a gulch, the posse positioned itself on the opposite bank about five hundred yards away. A rifleman's bullet hit Bass's cartridge belt and another splintered the stock of his rifle. Startled but undaunted, Bass led the Rangers on another chase around the hills before losing them in the green labyrinth.

After lolling amidst the cedars in Stephens County for a couple of weeks, the gang leader was soon ready for another chase. Into the small towns the gang stormed like large twisters, loud, disruptive, furiously spending San Francisco mint pieces on liquor and other necessities and then away again, taunting their pursuers.

In Wise County, Bass led the gang into another precarious position. This time one of his men was killed along with some of the horses. Several gang members decided to leave Sam after the Wise County shootout, concluding that Bass was more interested in achieving fame by dodging his chasers than by pulling off new robberies. The Bass War, they figured, had deteriorated into a wild game of chase, a game in which they were sure to run out of escapes.

In the spring of 1878, police authorities around Denton decided on a dragnet and arrested on the slightest whim a number of citizens suspected of abetting Sam Bass. One of those taken into custody was a man named Jim Murphy, a longtime acquaintance of Sam. When they brought in Jim Murphy, they shortened Sam's days.

In his breathless chases with lawmen, in his quest for

headlines, with that apparent immunity to real fear of being killed that characterized the most notable bandit kings, in his supreme effort to establish a particular identity that would be remembered and respected—in all these things, Bass tried to measure up to Jesse James. To some folks in Texas, he became as legendary as Jesse. After all, the man created a "war" on his own. Just like someone did for Jesse, a writer composed a ballad telling of Sam's life. Folks compared him to Robin Hood. Sam Bass—"The Texas Robin Hood." Never mind the record—one fabulous score at Big Springs and a succession of holdups notable only for their futility. Sam Bass was an original, they said, a poor sodbustin' kid who had made the feds, the Pinkertons, and the train and stage companies all red faced, a kid who had distinguished himself.

But Sam Bass, in his headlong rush to notoriety, achieved parity with the greatest bandit figures only in one deadly respect—he let someone he knew get too close. Jesse had been shot in the back. Years later, Dillinger let one woman too many into his confidence. For Sam, it was Jim Murphy.

While in jail in Tyler, Texas, in May 1878, Murphy decided to save himself further time behind bars and to pick up some reward money. In a written agreement with U.S. District Attorney Andrew Evans, Murphy agreed to a plot to lure Bass and the other gang members into "a position where they could be captured." When Sam and another gang member stopped by Murphy's home and asked him to join in their next mission—a bank robbery, place as yet undecided—Murphy set the trap.

In the weeks following, Murphy looked for a chance to initiate the plan. Even though a couple of the gang members had been informed through outlaw connections that Murphy might be in league with lawmen or on the make for reward money, Sam wouldn't listen to any of their warnings. Jim Murphy was an old, loyal friend.

On July 13, 1878, Sam, Murphy, and the rest of the gang rode into Belton, Texas, on their way to rob the bank in Round

Rock, in Williamson County. Murphy managed to leave the rest of the gang in Belton for enough time to send a letter to federal marshals and the county sheriff alerting them to the gang's target. In a later wire to Major Jones, Murphy said that if the lawmen weren't in Round Rock "I would have to help them rob the bank or a train or they would kill me . . . for God's sake, get there."

On Sunday, July 14, the bandits reached Round Rock in time to take a look at the bank and the layout of the town. Next morning, the brash plotters walked the streets, stopped in for a shave at the barbershop, and looked around for fresh horses that might be available for the escape. Instead of stealing new horses, Bass decided to keep the boys in town for a few days, rest their own horses, and hit the bank on the afternoon of July 20.

Jim Murphy's letters reached their destinations. Into Round Rock rode several Texas Rangers disguised as cowboys. On Friday, the day before the scheduled hit, saying he would hang around outside of town to keep an eye open for lawmen, Jim Murphy separated from the others. Round Rock, Texas, was ready for its own piece of bandit history.

In an alley next to Koppel's grocery store, Bass and two of his buddies tied their horses. When they entered the store a deputy sheriff named A. W. Grimes, accompanied by another lawman, followed them inside. Sam and the other outlaws blasted the lawmen and Grimes crumpled. As the outlaws desperately raced outside for their horses, the roar and smell and the smoke and dust of gunfire surrounded them. One of the gang members fell dead, his head shattered; Bass, hit in the stomach, managed to climb onto one of the horses with another of the gang, Frank Jackson. Bass didn't get far out of town. He told Jackson to leave him off on the side of the road; the ride was too painful. The next day searchers found Bass lying by an oak tree, nearly dead.

The Rangers took him to an empty shack in Round Rock, laid him on a cot, and began to grill him with questions. Bass refused to give them any answers. Major Jones later remem-

ANOTHER LEGEND

His real name was Charles E. Boles; his monicker was "Black Bart." He was the country's most celebrated stagecoach robber. Between 1875 and 1883, the dapper bandit, wearing a long linen duster, a flour sack over his head, and wielding a shotgun, held up dozens of stages, mostly in California, without firing a shot. At the scene of one of his Wells Fargo robberies, Bart left this note:

I've labored long and hard for bread,
For honor and for riches,
But on my corns too long you've tread,
You fine haired sons of bitches.

(Wells Fargo Bank)

ABOVE: A Wells Fargo Express Company "Treasure Wagon," one of the targets of Black Bart and other stage robbers.
(Library of Congress, LC-USZ62-11769)

LEFT: Deadwood Dick, stagecoach driver.
(National Archives, 111-SC-94118)

bered: "I tried every conceivable plan to obtain some information from him, but to no purpose. About noon on Sunday he began to suffer greatly and sent for me to know if I could not give him some relief. I did everything I could for him." The major also continued to try to get information. According to Jones, Bass said, "It is against my profession to blow on my pals. If a man knows anything he ought to die with it in him." Bass did just that.

Sam Bass died on July 21, 1878. It was his birthday. None of the great bandits, not Jesse or Dillinger, not Pretty Boy or Butch, died on their birthdays. Sam might not have been much of a bandit but he had in him the stuff of legends.

4

COFFEYVILLE

Violence on the frontier—the end of a shootout in Hays, Kansas, leaves two dead.

(Kansas State Historical Society)

THEY TRIED TO DO WHAT JESSE JAMES AND THE YOUNGERS HAD NEVER DONE. THEY TRIED TO SET THEIR OWN STANDARD BY WHICH OUTLAW HEROES WOULD BE JUDGED. THEY TRIED TO ROB TWO BANKS AT THE SAME TIME.

The Dalton gang—Emmett, Grat, and Bob; cousins of the Youngers; sons of Adeline Younger Dalton, a half sister of Colonel Henry Younger—this was a gang with a bandit heritage. There were eight brothers in the Dalton family. Three became farmers and remained farmers; one, Frank, became a deputy marshal and died in the line of duty; three started the Dalton gang after being deputies for a time; one became a politician and, later, also became an outlaw. The outlaw Daltons saw themselves as kings of the second generation of outlaws.

Grat Dalton was born in 1862, a year before Quantrill's sack of Lawrence; Bob in 1867, a year after the Reno brothers began robbing trains in Indiana; and Emmett in 1871, during the glory days of the James gang. The boys lived for a while near Coffeyville, Kansas, where Civil War guerrillas had roamed and terrorized; they also lived in Missouri, haunt of the James boys. They later moved to the

The C. M. Condon & Co. Bank of Coffeyville, Kansas, one of the two targets the Dalton gang planned to hit on the same day.

(Coffeyville Historical Society)

wild lands of Indian Territory, where aspiring train and bank robbers vied for attention and spoils. The Daltons knew all about marauding and outlawry.

The Dalton family had lost property in the Civil War, and the boys spent their early years listening to their father, Louis, and their mother reminiscing about balmy days past. The boys also grew up hearing stories about their cousins, the Youngers, and about Jesse and Frank, friends of their cousins.

Four of the brothers tried the other side of the law, working for the U.S. marshal's office in the Western District of Arkansas in Fort Smith, the province of Judge Isaac Parker, whose influence ranged over several thousand miles and whose personal appellation as "the hanging judge" was well earned. The judge often presided over two or three hangings at a time.

Grat, Bob, and Emmett served as deputies, along with Frank, the brother who did not survive his law enforcement career. Jacob Yoes, a United States marshal in Arkansas, remembered the brothers as "good and fearless officers," remembered a week when the boys tracked down fugitives from a Little Rock prison and brought them in. Although young, the Daltons had been, said Marshal Yoes, promising lawmen. A schoolteacher also remembered the boys as "nice and polite."

Soon, however, the reputations of the Daltons began a metamorphism. The pay of deputy marshals was low and erratic. Bob began to supplement his income by dabbling in shady deals with land grabbers. Grat was arrested in Tulsa on drunkenness charges and "conducting himself badly." More seriously, on September 6, 1890, warrants were served on Bob and Emmett for horse theft. The boys later said that they had turned to crime because the federal government had not paid them for their services. The names of the Daltons thus shifted to the other side of the ledger.

The two most prominent bandit gangs—the James-Younger gang and the Dalton gang—were rooted in kinship, organized around sets of brothers, supported by relatives and friends who felt them to be compatriots. If the Jameses and Youngers had many ex-Confederate connections who shielded them, the Daltons had many friends among the farmers and ranchers along the Cimarron River. Some of the Daltons' allies were active in selling stolen goods; others were simply friends of the large family. The outlaw Daltons even attended community events in Oklahoma in times when their capture promised hefty rewards. The men had made friends who predated their criminal careers. In a time and place in which the differences between law breakers and law enforcers were sometimes difficult to discern, many of the friendships established by the Daltons endured. Only when the Daltons seemed to threaten the community itself and not merely the railroad companies, institutions many ranchers and farmers despised, did the community turn against the gang.

When the boys ventured into unfamiliar areas of the country, they faced greater odds. In early 1891, the gang members heard that the Southern Pacific line from Los Angeles to San Francisco carried hundreds of rich tourists and express cars loaded with small fortunes and that the Southern Pacific Company had advertised that the run was free from the desperado pestilence contaminating railway travel elsewhere. For the Daltons, this was a challenge that offered both notoriety and riches. But after the boys robbed a train near Alila, California, in early February, Grat was arrested. Later, on a train headed for the state penitentiary, he managed to escape. Concluding that California was not their natural habitat, the boys returned to the familiar lands of Kansas and Oklahoma.

In June 1892, shortly after Bob Ford, the murderer of Jesse James, was gunned down in a honky-tonk saloon in Creede, Colorado, the Daltons hit a Texas Express train near Red Rock in the Cherokee Strip. They took over other trains successfully, always managing to pick lucrative express cars. Much of the credit for their string of cash payoffs was due to the advance work of Bob's fiancée, Eugenia Moore. Posing as a lady inquiring about sending large express shipments of banknotes, Eugenia was often able to learn from railroad dispatchers and other officials the identities of the trains with the richest hauls.

The gang developed its own trademark. Wearing masks and carrying Winchesters, they entered a train depot, subdued the employees, ransacked the office of its money and valuables, and cut the telegraph wires. When the train entered the station, the gang members swung aboard, some to take over the controls of the train, the others to break into the express car. They did not rob the passengers. When the contents of the express car had been secured, they rode away, riddling the sides of the train with bullets. They split off in separate directions to confuse their pursuers.

Federal marshals, vigilance committees, bounty hunters, and posses hired by express companies and railroads fanned out through Oklahoma (Indian Territory) to bring down the Daltons—rewards of up to $5,000 a man. U.S. Deputy Marshal Ransom Payne was especially intent, reminding some of his colleagues of a slavering wolf on the trail. Despite his intensity, he didn't get close.

Some newspaper editorialists were now suggesting that the Daltons could become even greater than the Jameses and the Youngers. Brash and arrogant, Bob Dalton became the clan leader despite his youth. He began to believe all the hyperbole about bandit heroes and about the rise of the Daltons to the heights. In the fall of 1892, as he and his brothers attended a family reunion in Fort Smith, Arkansas, Bob hatched a scheme designed to dwarf the hallowed images of Jesse and the others, a plan that, if executed, could propel the Daltons to bandit immortality. The gang, Bob believed, could turn its train-robbing skills to banks—and not just one bank at a time.

Coffeyville, Kansas, was a relatively new town, established shortly after the Civil War on the banks of the Verdigris River near the Oklahoma line. In its infancy it was a wild hangout for bootleggers peddling illegal whiskey in Indian Territory, but it had mellowed over the years. The Daltons had lived in Coffeyville for a time, but despite their success, some of the local residents had made disparaging remarks about the boys, had not taken them to heart as heroic figures or local boys who had made it big. Bob Dalton resented the rebuffs of some of his former neighbors.

Coffeyville now had a number of thriving businesses and was on the line of three separate railroads. It also had two prosperous banks, the First National, on Union Street, and the C. M. Condon Company, across the street on the north side of the plaza.

On the morning of October 5, 1892, the Daltons—Bob, Grat, and Emmett—accompanied by veteran bandits Dick Broadwell and Bill Powers, rode into town. The group did not include a tough bandit named Bill Doolin, who had been involved in the plans. Bill's horse went lame before the attack, or at least that's what he claimed. Some people later suggested that Bill had seen the folly of this whole enterprise and had chosen discretion over suicide. Bill Doolin would thus survive this day to form his own gang.

The five who rode into Coffeyville that morning wore fake mustaches and whiskers and were heavily armed. Turning onto Maple Street and then down an alley, the gang dismounted and tied their horses to a fence. The pathetic disguises didn't work. Several townspeople recognized the boys, and word began to spread.

As Bob and Emmett entered the lobby of the First National, and Grat, Powers, and Broadwell walked into the Condon, several townsmen rushed to the hardware store for rifles. Bob and Emmett, clutching a feed bag filled with about $20,000, were the first to reach the street, using three bank employees as shields. As the other gang members left the First National, Coffeyville, Kansas, erupted—bullets ringing off the bank walls and smashing through the windows; terrified hostages falling to the ground and scrambling for cover; storekeepers, clerks, farmers, a town carpenter, and a harness maker forming a small army blocking the escape. Like the James gang at Northfield, the Daltons were engulfed in the crossfire of blazing Winchesters and six-guns. Small puffs of dust jumped from the bandits' coats as bullets ripped into them.

They made it into the alley. Soon, it would be called "Death Alley." As the wounded bandits tried to mount their horses, they were quickly trapped by men advancing down both ends of the alley, filling the small enclosure with a withering

Grat Dalton, at age of 24. He was 33 when
killed at Coffeyville,Kan.,Oct.5,1892.

Grat Dalton, age twenty-four, seven years before the Coffeyville robbery attempt.

(Arizona Historical Society/Tucson)

fire, a horrifying fusillade of bullets ricocheting off walls, puncturing men and horses. The owner of a livery stable, a man named John Kloehr, one of the town's best shots, maneuvered himself behind the fence where the gang had tied the horses, a position only a few feet from Bob Dalton's back. As Kloehr aimed, Bob whirled, only to take the shot in the stomach. The gang leader toppled backward and died. Grat Dalton quickly took aim at Kloehr but also became a victim. Kloehr shot him through the throat.

Grabbing the money sack, the wounded Emmett lurched crazily toward the end of the alley, only to see a lifeless Bill Powers falling face first into the dirt. A few seconds later, Dick Broadwell spun out of his saddle onto Maple Street, another fatality. Only Emmett, among the gang members, still breathed. A barber named Carey Seamen had shot Emmett in the legs and hip, and the last of the Dalton gang sprawled over in the street. As Emmett writhed on the

"Death Alley" in Coffeyville where the Dalton gang was exterminated.

(Kansas State Historical Society)

A bullet-marked bank shows the scars of the fierce battle in Coffeyville.

(Coffeyville Historical Society)

ground, the shooting stopped, with clouds of smoke choking onlookers and the bodies of bandits and Coffeyville citizens and horses lying in disarray.

People snippped off locks of Bob's hair; poked at the holes in the bodies; stood them upright for the benefit of a photographer; moved them into various positions, finally side by side into the pose that in books and periodicals and newspapers would come to represent the violence, the suddenness of extermination, the repulsion, and the fascination with the lives and the deaths of those in America's gun culture. Four men stared vacantly in Coffeyville, stopped finally and surely, no longer menacing or heroic, no longer anything.

Emmett Dalton lay in an upstairs room in a small boardinghouse called the Farmer's Home. Nursing his wounded legs, right hip, right arm, and his back, which had absorbed a dozen buckshot, he told a reporter from the *Kansas City Star* about the Coffeyville disaster, about Bob Dalton's plan to elevate the status of the gang in the history of bank robbing: "Bob said he wanted to lower Jesse James's record. I tried to persuade him not to try it, but did not succeed, as he had a grudge against the town and wanted revenge for what he had heard the people here were saying and trying to do about us."

There was some talk among the citizenry about lynching Emmett, but that seemed somewhat ridiculous since doctors gave him only a few hours to live. There was some talk about amputating his wounded arm, but Emmett refused. Over the next few days, the Coffeyville shootout did not, as most people had expected, claim another life. Emmett improved. Sent to prison in Lansing, Kansas, for life, he was later pardoned.

In Coffeyville, the Dalton brothers had tried to achieve a status rivaling their cousins. The irony is that in Coffeyville, like the Youngers in Northfield, the brother gang was obliterated by townspeople.

Lawmen were generally pleased with the outcome. Chris Madsen, chief deputy of the U.S. marshal's office in Oklahoma, believed that killing the boys was the only answer: "It may be noticed that all of those men are either mere boys or young men, and I believe that not one of them ever reached the age of thirty years; but the crimes committed by them have been second to none committed by their class, and they have been a source of annoyance to this country for a long time. They have cost the Government, as well as the officers here, great amounts of money and time, and would have cost a great deal more had they lived long enough to get a trial instead of going down as they did." But Deputy Marshal Red Orrington called the Daltons "as fine fellows as I ever knew." They turned to banditry, Red said, for "love of adventure."

In California, Bill Dalton, a man who had gone straight, who had dabbled in state politics and nurtured further political ambitions, rushed to Kansas when he heard the news about his brothers. Because of the notoriety, his political

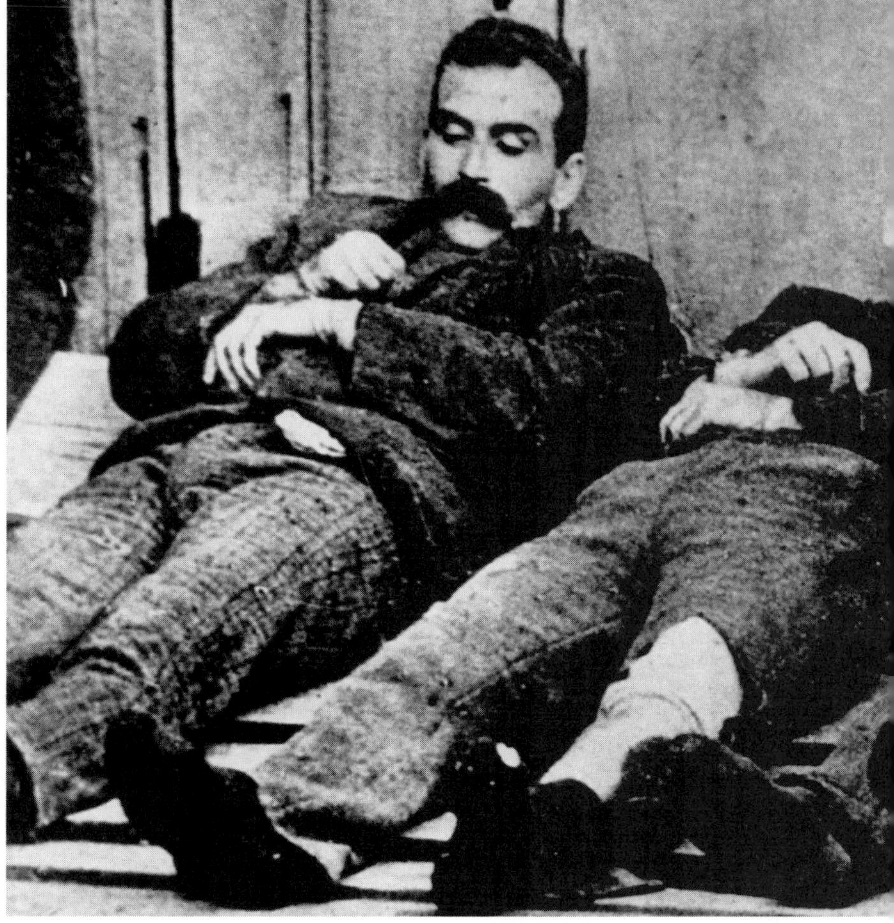

Coffeyville fatalities—Bill Powers, Bob and Grat Dalton, and Dick Broadwell.

(National Archives, 111-SC-93378)

career, he knew, was ruined. Bill decided on revenge. He joined a bandit gang headed by Bill Doolin, the Dalton gang member who had not ridden into Coffeyville with his friends.

Emmett Dalton walked out of prison in 1907 after serving fifteen years of a twenty-five-year sentence. He wrote two books: *Beyond the Law* and *When the Daltons Rode,* the latter with help from a Sacramento, California, reporter. The books, he said, testified to the futility of a life of crime.

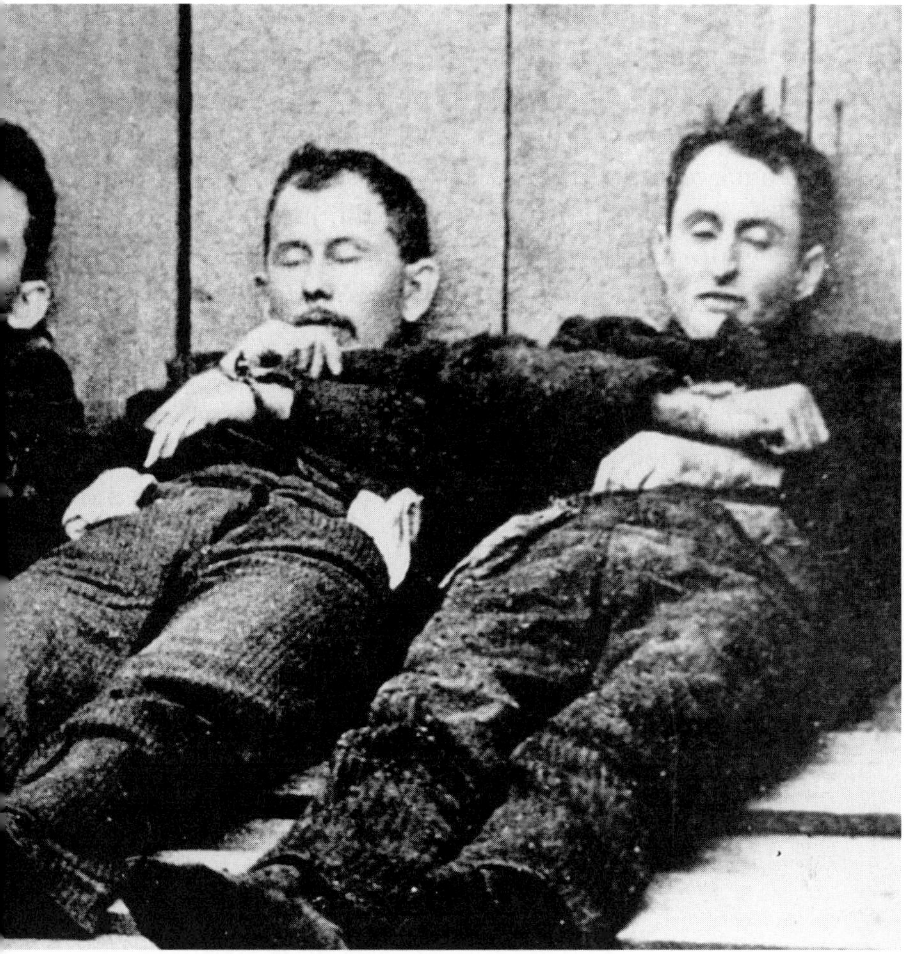

He also made a movie in Hollywood.

In May 1931 he returned to Coffeyville "to go over the old trails." Standing at the foot of the graves of Grat and Bob and Bill Powers, Emmett said to a reporter, "I challenge the world to produce the history of an outlaw who ever got anything out of it but that or else be huddled in a prison cell. . . ." This was a different age of banditry, said Emmett, but the lessons were still the same. "The machine gun may help them get away with it a little better and the motorcar may help them in making an escape better than to ride on horseback, as we did, but it all ends the same way." Emmett Dalton outlived John Dillinger.

In Coffeyville today, tourists can still see "Death Alley,"

can see the Condon & Company bank, and the old stone jail, and can see the graves of the gang members in Elmwood Cemetery. At 113 East Eighth Street, the Dalton Museum stands adjacent to the alley where Bob and Emmett raced from the back of First National. The museum was established in 1954. It features exhibits on historical figures who lived in the Coffeyville area, especially baseball pitcher Walter Johnson and presidential candidate Wendell Willkie. Its focus, nevertheless, is on the Dalton gang, with photographs and relics from that grisly day over a century ago. The 1954 committee that assembled to create the museum was headed by a man named Kloehr. One of his relatives from an earlier generation had owned a livery stable and had been a crack shot.

5

THE INGALLS RAID

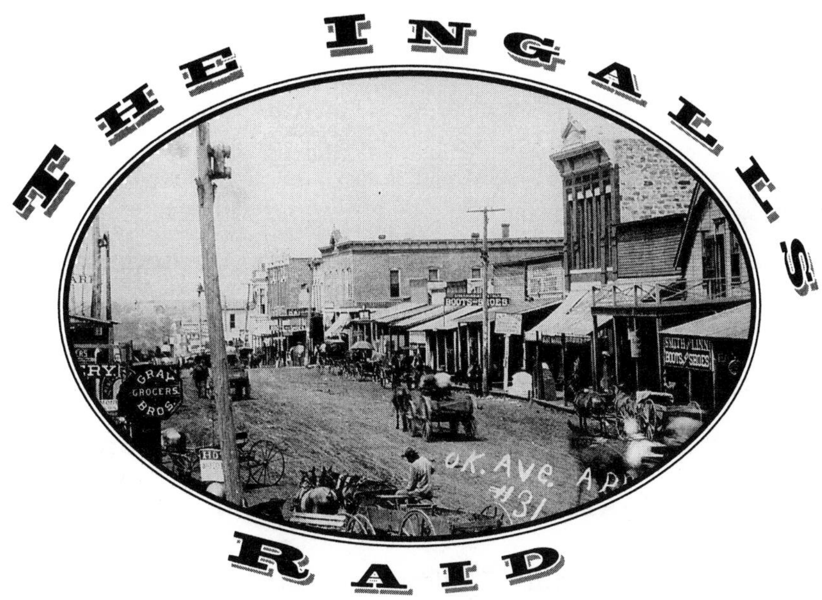

Oklahoma Avenue, Guthrie, Oklahoma, April 1893.

(National Archives, 48-RST-7B31)

THE CIVIL WAR MADE MANY SMALL TOWNS FAMOUS—GETTYSBURG, PENNSYLVANIA; CHANCELLORSVILLE, VIRGINIA; VICKSBURG, MISSISSIPPI. FOLLOWING THE WAR, BANDITS GAVE A MEASURE OF NOTORIETY TO OTHER SMALL TOWNS—NORTHFEILD, MINNESOTA;

Glendale, Missouri; Coffeyville, Kansas. And then, in September 1893, Ingalls, Oklahoma.

Located four miles west of the territorial border, Ingalls got its first post office in January 1890. It could boast of a few stores, some saloons, one hotel, a few livery barns, and about five doctors. It also had a band of outlaws who had chosen the community as a hangout. They played poker, drank in the saloons, made friends with many of the residents, brought in oysters for the country dances, even occasionally gave money to the preacher. When they left town for a period, no one asked where they had gone; when they returned flush with cash no one asked where they had been.

One of the residents of Ingalls in 1893 was a girl named Rose who lived at the Dunn Ranch, southeast of town. Rose was about fifteen years old—a beauty, it was said. Rumor had it that she had taken up with one of the outlaws, a man named "Bitter Creek," a tough gun-

Wild West Hotel, Calamity Avenue, Perry, Oklahoma, 1893.

(National Archives, 49-AR-22)

fighter who often stayed at Mary Pierce's O.K. Hotel. Years later, after the events that occurred in Ingalls in September 1893, writers from the East, storytellers, even poets, began to tell the tale of "Cimarron Rose." Grover Leonard, the Cowboy Poet of Oklahoma, left these words:

Rose of the Cimarron, Bitter Creek's girl,
Stood watching the dancers glide and whirl.
The dance grows wilder, they're young, don't you see?
"Gosh," says Red Buck, "so were we!"

The Cowboy Poet and others gave Rose and Bitter Creek

and Ingalls a bandit identity after 1893. It was said by many that Rose had married Bitter Creek. It was said that she was in a saloon with Bitter Creek on that famous day in Ingalls. It was said that when he was wounded in the leg, she slid down from a room in the O.K. Hotel on knotted bedsheets carrying Bitter Creek's Winchester and ammunition and rushed to his side. It was said that Bitter Creek and Cimarron Rose were in love and that she followed him on his wanderings and even tried to get him to stop drinking. One writer called Rose "the most reckless woman bandit of Oklahoma." The only thing reckless with all of this had been the facts. But because of Grover Leonard, Rose of the Cimarron became etched in outlaw lore.

* * * * * * *

If Glendale is remembered for Jesse; if Northfield is remembered for the James boys and the Youngers; if Coffeyville is remembered for the Daltons; then Ingalls is remembered for the Doolin gang.

Shadows of dead men stand by the wall
Watching the fun of the pioneer ball.
The wail of fiddles, the dancers sway—
Troubles forgotten for a night and a day.

Born in Johnson County, Arkansas, just before the Civil War, Bill Doolin, son of a sharecropper, drifted into Indian Territory in the early 1880s. After spending several years herding cattle, Doolin became a ranch foreman. While working at the Halsell Ranch on the Cimarron River, he made friends with Bitter Creek Newcomb, Dick Broadwell, Bill Powers, and others who would drift from the cowboy life into the outlaw business. For a time Doolin made extra money selling whiskey to the Indians.

In 1889, Oklahoma Territory was organized and many large ranches lost much of their rangeland. Some cowboys lost jobs, and some, such as Bill Doolin, turned to outlawry.

On the Fourth of July 1890, Doolin was on the run after a shooting incident in which two lawmen were wounded. Doolin soon hooked up with the Dalton gang, but because of his supposed lame horse, Bill was not with the gang in Coffeyville on October 5, 1892. He was fortunate.

After learning of the events in Coffeyville and the deaths of Broadwell and Powers and all of the Daltons except Emmett, Doolin decided to form his own gang. He recruited men from Oklahoma, and the gang took on the name the "Oklahombres." Doolin also persuaded a variety of gunmen from other parts of the West to join on—Jack Blake ("Tulsa Jack"), Roy Daugherty ("Arkansas Tom Jones"), and George Waightman ("Red Buck"). Old-timers said that Red Buck would kill anyone for $50; just hand the man $50 and point out the victim.

Doolin also recruited two other men who had ridden at times with the Dalton gang—Bitter Creek Newcomb and Charley Pierce. Newcomb, a drifter who had herded cows in Texas and Oklahoma, was the most riotous of the Dalton gang. During the Daltons' drunken celebrations after successful raids, Newcomb often sang:

I'M A WILD WOLF FROM BITTER CREEK,
AND IT'S MY NIGHT TO HOWL!

The moniker stuck. Bitter Creek Newcomb would no longer howl with the Daltons but he now had the Doolin bunch.

Charley Pierce was also a former cowboy. Charley had become entranced with the stories about Bill Quantrill and about the James boys and had turned to burglary and whiskey and then to smuggling before hooking up with the Daltons. Doolin had put together a formidable bunch. And then he added a Dalton.

Bill Dalton, the Dalton brother who had not been a member of the ill-fated gang, had resisted the raider life, had even begun a political career in the West. But Bill Dalton's future had been hopelessly compromised because of the sordid reputation of his kinfolk. He finally decided to seek family revenge. But Dalton's outlaw career would be short-lived.

Dan Clifton, sporting the moniker "Dynamite Dick," also joined up. Dick's name derived from his practice of drilling holes in his Winchester bullets, filling them with dynamite, and plugging the holes with lead. When the loaded bullets struck, they exploded.

Romping through Oklahoma Territory, the gang robbed banks, stages, and trains and soon became a prime target for hired Pinkertons and marshals. In the spring of 1893 Doolin was wounded in the foot following a robbery. In Ingalls he sought treatment from Dr. Duncan Selph, who dug numerous bone particles out of his flesh. The gang leader also sought comfort in the arms of Edith Ellsworth, whom he had secretly married in Kingfisher, Oklahoma, in March. Edith, now pregnant, lived in the O.K. Hotel, where she helped out her good friend, Mary Pierce.

The gang stayed in Ingalls for the summer as Doolin's foot healed. On one occasion, several citizens in Ingalls reported seeing Marshal Heck Thomas in town. Later, two federal officers rode into Ingalls disguised as land surveyors. They stayed for a while, drank, and played cards with the various gang members. They reported back to the marshals that the gang was in Ingalls, was unprepared for an assault, and was ripe for the taking.

Federal marshals in the West were constantly battling a plethora of problems in dealing with the outlaw menace. They were frustrated by the prospect of mustering competent posses when they could offer only minimal pay for extremely hazardous work. They were also frustrated by the potent challenge of outlaw gangs like the Doolin bunch. This was a group of men who knew the countryside, who controlled much of the population, and who had excellent horses and full arsenals accumulated through various deals and thefts. It was a group who had a "nothing to lose" mentality and whose quest for notoriety was driven by the heroic images painted in stories told by veteran hustlers and gang members in bars and around campfires all over Oklahoma and by cheap novels they passed around.

Bill Grimes, a U.S. marshal from Oklahoma, blamed the outlaw phenomenon on the economic dislocation of the West, which found many out-of-work cowboys and drifters like Bill Doolin looking for itinerant jobs. He also blamed the atmosphere, where the young fellows' "heads have been turned by reading dime novels while spending their winters in idleness far away from civilization, and in their camps where old desperadoes come and relate their doings into crime even before they were of age."

Another federal marshal, Evett Nix of Guthrie, Oklahoma, talked about how the community shielded the gangs, how the Doolin gang, like the James brothers and the Daltons, had cultivated a large, loyal following in their home regions, an almost impenetrable network of protection: "the inhabitants of that part of the Territory infested by them are either on friendly terms with them or they have been so terrorized and intimidated by threats against their lives and destruction of their property, that they dare not and do not volunteer the slightest information, or take any step that would lead to the discovery of the acts, whereabouts, or intentions of the outlaws."

The undersheriff of Pawnee County, Frank Canton, spent many long days in futile pursuit of the Doolin gang. He later wrote of the gang's many friends along the Cimarron River, farmers, ranchers, many honest citizens who protected the outlaws even at risk to themselves. "There is no doubt," Canton wrote, "that Doolin furnished many of them money to buy groceries to live upon when they first settled in that country . . ." They gave in return their loyalty. "Even though he was an outlaw with a price on his head . . . there were plenty of people who would get up at the hour of midnight if necessary to ride to Bill Doolin to warn him of the approach of officers." Years later, in the Cooksin Hills area of Oklahoma, law enforcement officials would echo the same complaints about the hill folk who shielded

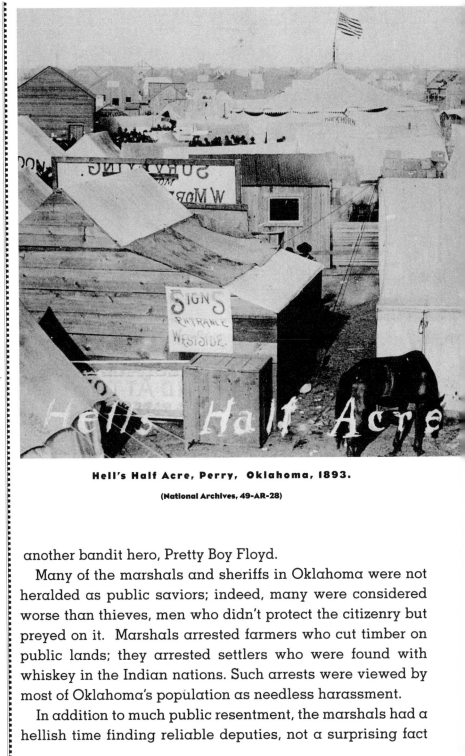

Hell's Half Acre, Perry, Oklahoma, 1893.

(National Archives, 49-AR-28)

another bandit hero, Pretty Boy Floyd.

Many of the marshals and sheriffs in Oklahoma were not heralded as public saviors; indeed, many were considered worse than thieves, men who didn't protect the citizenry but preyed on it. Marshals arrested farmers who cut timber on public lands; they arrested settlers who were found with whiskey in the Indian nations. Such arrests were viewed by most of Oklahoma's population as needless harassment.

In addition to much public resentment, the marshals had a hellish time finding reliable deputies, not a surprising fact

considering the pay of two dollars a day to go up against hardened killers. One marshal remarked, "It takes men of nerves and men who have little concern, so far as comfort and emoluments are concerned, to take the trail after such men." In other words, it took men whose natures were very similar to those of the criminals themselves. Indeed, many men crossed over from time to time, changing roles depending on personal considerations and circumstances. The Daltons—Grat, Bob, and Emmett—had, for example, all been employed, at one time or another, by marshals in the West District of Arkansas.

This fact was not lost to Missouri Senator George G. Vest. The western territories were a menace to civilization, the senator charged in a speech on the floor of Congress; crime was rampant, corruption rife, the area "filled with criminals who have fled from justice . . . and who laugh at the courts . . ." The senator talked of the Daltons, the banditti who had rampaged through the west robbing and killing until they were stopped at Coffeyville. "Monstrous as the proposition is," Vest declared, "these Dalton brothers . . . had been deputy marshals of the United States. . . . I assert here now from reliable authority that the lawless classes . . . have furnished a large number of the officers of the United States employed as deputy marshals within that jurisdiction."

Despite the senator's ravings, the two marshals planning to take the Doolin gang in Ingalls were not, and never had been, of the lawless classes; instead, they were two of the most frustrated law enforcement officials in the country, faced with the ominous daily challenge of dealing with men such as Arkansas Tom and Dynamite Dick. The two, Deputy Marshal John Hixon and Deputy Marshal Heck Thomas, veteran bandit chasers in Indian Territory, devised an unusual strategy to take the gang. Although Thomas had favored his own trusted method of infiltrating the enemy camp with one or a few snipers, he finally agreed with Hixon's idea to outfit two covered wagons, fill them with heavily armed posse members, and roll into Ingalls, inconspicuously blending in with other covered wagons around town.

An advance scout for the posse, who was sent ahead to assess matters, reported to Hixon that all the gang members were in George Ransom's saloon. The advance scout was wrong and his error would prove to be disastrous.

In Ingalls, the citizenry, always vigilant in warning the Doolin bunch of any plans they had heard regarding upcoming posse raids or actual sightings of law enforcement officials, had been on the job again. When the marshals' plot to raid Ingalls was hatched, an informer got the message to Doolin. The gang was prepared.

On the morning of September 1, 1893, the two wagons quietly rolled into Ingalls, mixing with other wagons in town. As the first wagon slowly ground to a halt in front of Light's Black Smith Shop, the other moved up the street toward Ransom's saloon, where most, but not all, of the Doolin gang members were downing whiskey and playing cards. As some of the posse climbed down to take positions near the saloon, Bitter Creek stepped outside. Seeing several men carrying guns, obviously the posse, he wheeled to fire, but a bullet hit the magazine of his Winchester and the blast gouged a wound in his thigh.

From an attic room in the O.K. Hotel, Arkansas Tom, in perfect sniper position, had a splendid view of the unfolding war below. His Winchester was soon winging bullets at the enemy. The old cowpuncher from Texas and Oklahoma managed to fell the deputy who had shot Bitter Creek and then trained his sights on other targets. He shot a fourteen-year-old boy by mistake. He shot a horse and disintegrated a chicken. Tom's withering, if wanton, firing proved a great distraction for the lawmen trying to trap the gang in the saloon.

Badly outnumbered, however, the Doolin bunch soon found itself in desperate trouble as the lawmen's fire splintered some of the wooden building, the construction of which was never intended to withstand a relentless barrage of rifle and shotgun fire. The barkeeper, George Ransom, trying to shield himself amidst the rubble, was hit in the leg. The five outlaws, returning the posse's fire with a respectable rain of bullets of their own, were not even nicked. But with their position becoming increasingly precarious, the gang managed, through the smoke, flames, and confusion, to make their way out of a side door and into the stable nearby where their horses waited.

While Doolin, Dynamite, Dalton, Red Buck, and Tulsa Jack scrambled into the stable to mount up, marshals quickly closed in, shattering their newest target, the stable, just as easily as they had shattered the saloon. Through all of the shelling, nevertheless, only Bitter Creek among the gang members had sustained an injury. Meanwhile, Arkansas Tom, standing on a chair, was still firing away from the O.K. Hotel attic. He picked off one of the posse crouching behind a lumber pile.

As the posse poured more lead into the stable, the five gang members charged out, defying the streams of bullets, and headed off. Dalton's horse, hit in the jaw and then in a leg, went down in agony. Unhurt by the animal's fall, Dalton raced toward safety in a ravine bordering Ingalls only to find a member of the posse, Deputy Lafe Shadley, blocking his path, ready to blast him away. Dalton was saved from above. Arkansas Tom picked off another victim.

Dalton and the wounded Bitter Creek both found mounts in

the confusion and joined the others in a wild race to the prairie. In the rush for freedom Dynamite Dick was hit in the neck, a wound from which he would recover.

The gang had been saved by one of their brethren who was now in a very precarious position. As some of the posse gave chase to his friends, Arkansas Tom now found himself the lone target of the rest of the lawmen in town. Bullets crashed through the attic, blasting away almost everything in the room except the outlaw. During a lull in the firing, the marshals threatened to burn down the hotel with him in it. Arkansas Tom gave up.

At his trial in the courtroom of federal judge Frank Dale, Tom seemed chagrined that the rest of the gang had deserted him, that the fact that he had saved most of their lives seemed to matter little. Most residents of Ingalls and the surrounding territory had assumed that the Doolin gang would try to rescue Tom from his predicament in the weeks following the shootout; Tom had thought so too. They had not. And now Tom sat there at the defendant's table, with a dozen armed guards outside preparing for any contingency, a disappointed outlaw. Somehow, the code had been forgotten; somehow the Doolin bunch seemed to Tom less honorable, less formidable. Somehow, the mystique had been lost.

Convicted of first-degree manslaughter, Arkansas Tom spent nearly the rest of his life in the Lansing Michigan federal penitentiary—and he lived until 1924, long after the rest of his comrades had perished. He remained an outlaw to the end, killed by officers in Joplin, Missouri, while evading arrest for another bank robbery.

To Judge Dale, however, the testimony given by law enforcement officials and residents of Ingalls had been a shocking revelation of the dangers posed by western outlaws. Their glorification in song and ballad and dime novel was an affront to civilized society, their success a menace to the maintenance of order on the frontier. Following the trial, Dale called one of the marshals to his chambers. What the marshals faced, Dale said, was nothing less than a war against hardened combat veterans inured to senseless killing. The marshal later remembered Dale's words: "This is serious. I have reached the conclusion that the only good outlaw is a dead one. I hope you will instruct your deputies in the future to bring them in dead." As the story of the western outlaw unfolded, Judge Dale's charge would be, in most cases, obeyed. It was especially true in the case of the Doolin gang.

The gang made some big hits in 1894, including a $40,000 haul from a bank in East Texas. And in the months following, desperate to end the Doolin menace, railroad, bank, and political figures assembled a posse of formidable talent led by Marshal Bill Tilghman, Jr.

Perhaps the most respected U.S. marshal in the West, Bill Tilghman had always cheated death. The story goes that shortly after Bill was born in Fort Dodge, Iowa, in 1854 a Sioux arrow slashed through the sleeve of his mother's blouse as she held him in her arms. As a youngster on the Midwestern prairie, he hunted buffalo. At age twenty-three he became a deputy sheriff under Charlie Bassett, the chief law enforcement official of infamous Dodge City, Kansas. He now shot men, not buffalo. Tilghman survived Dodge to become a deputy U.S. marshal in Oklahoma. And now he joined veteran outlaw chasers Chris Madsen and Heck Thomas on the hunt for the Doolin gang.

The three well-known marshals relentlessly tracked the gang over a thousand-square-mile area, a job made even more difficult by the fact that another gang, led by Bill Cook and his brother Jim, was also hitting banks and trains in Oklahoma at the same time. But in April 1895, after a train holdup along the Cimarron River, Madsen and his deputies killed Tulsa Jack. Shortly thereafter, Bitter Creek Newcomb and Charley Pierce were killed at the Dunn Ranch. And, at a ranch house near Ardmore, Oklahoma, Bill Dalton met his own Coffeyville, shot by Deputy Marshal Loss Hart. Of the bandit Dalton brothers, only Emmett still lived.

But much of the press, weary of past ineptitude of western

$5,000.00

REWARD

FOR CAPTURE

DEAD OR ALIVE

OF

BILL DOOLIN

NOTORIOUS ROBBER OF TRAINS AND BANKS

ABOUT 6 FOOT 2 INCHES TALL, LT. BROWN HAIR, DANGEROUS, ALWAYS HEAVILY ARMED.

IMMEDIATELY CONTACT THE

U.S. MARSHAL'S OFFICE, GUTHRIE, OKLAHOMA TER.

Federal marshals convinced their superiors in Washington that the apprehension of Bill Doolin was in the national interest in the amount of $5,000.

(National Archives, RG 60, Year Files)

law enforcement, was not lush with praise. The *Stillwater Gazette* declared that lawmen must have been relieved finally to kill Dalton because they had always "made it a practice to ride in the opposite direction from where he was every time they got him located."

By late 1895, three years after Ingalls, most of the Doolin gang had been shot to pieces. Doolin, nevertheless, had survived. On occasion, he hid out with his wife and new baby. In Eureka Springs, Arkansas, however, Tilghman caught up with the elusive bandit, cornered him in a bathhouse where he had gone to ease an increasingly painful rheumatism, and made the arrest. When Tilghman wired ahead that he had captured Doolin and was bringing him to Guthrie, Oklahoma, the story hit the press. Citizens for miles around Guthrie gathered to see the infamous outlaw, some five thousand people cheering wildly as he arrived at the train station. To some, the hero was not Tilghman; it was Doolin, around whose black career abundant stories and tales had been concocted.

Like other bandit heroes, Doolin had taken on an almost superhuman quality—his instinct for survival, his legendary escapes, his bravado, and his fearlessness. The *Ardmore State Herald* openly talked of Doolin and his gang's daring and courage, their honor and resolve, their kindnesses to benighted travelers, their chivalrous acts toward women, their paternal instincts toward children, and the Robin Hood romanticism of their acts of outlawry.

As many might have expected, the federal jail at Guthrie could not hold the likes of Bill Doolin. In July, Doolin and other prisoners subdued a couple of guards and made off in the night for the Oklahoma hills. But the jailbreak was Doolin's last legendary feat. On August 25, 1896, his odyssey ended. Near his wife's house in Lawson, Oklahoma, as he walked down the road, Doolin was riddled with buckshot by Marshal Heck Thomas and some other lawmen. The usual, customary treatment of a notorious dead outlaw ensued—Doolin's punctured body, carrying sixteen buckshot and two

Saloon in Ingalls, Oklahoma, shortly after the shootout.

(Western History Collections, University of Oklahoma Library)

Winchester balls, was stripped of its shirt and laid out for public view. Photographers gathered and recorded for the nation's press and posterity the end of another bandit folk hero. At the Summit View Cemetery in Guthrie, Oklahoma,

an ancient, rusty buggy axle covered Bill Doolin's burial spot.

* * * * * * *

Ingalls. The Doolin gang had made no daring bank robberies that day in Ingalls, had made no money. But they had survived a manhunt and had killed three lawmen. In outlaw lore, Ingalls remained identified with outlaw daring and law enforcement futility; with bandit heroes, outnumbered but not outwitted. The Doolin gang had been a source of both local pride and disgust, had been central to local history and legend; it had been part of community experience. A grocer in Stillwater with the coincidental name of Bill Dalton, no relation to the famous family, had even used the name to commercial advantage. In a newspaper advertisement for his store, grocer Dalton had announced: "Bill Dalton's Gang Are After You And If You Can Give Them A Trial You Will Be Convinced That They Keep The Freshest and Best Goods In The City At The Lowest Prices." The gang had been a source of identity, men from the community from whom the residents found vicarious excitement and in whom they recognized symbols of masculine power.

Ironically, Ingalls had sealed the fate of the Doolin gang in two very different respects. It had given the boys a permanent niche in outlaw history and lore; it had also marked them for extermination. Judge Dale's admonition had been serious advice, not hyperbole: Blow them away before the West succumbs to the anarchy of thugs; " . . . bring them in dead."

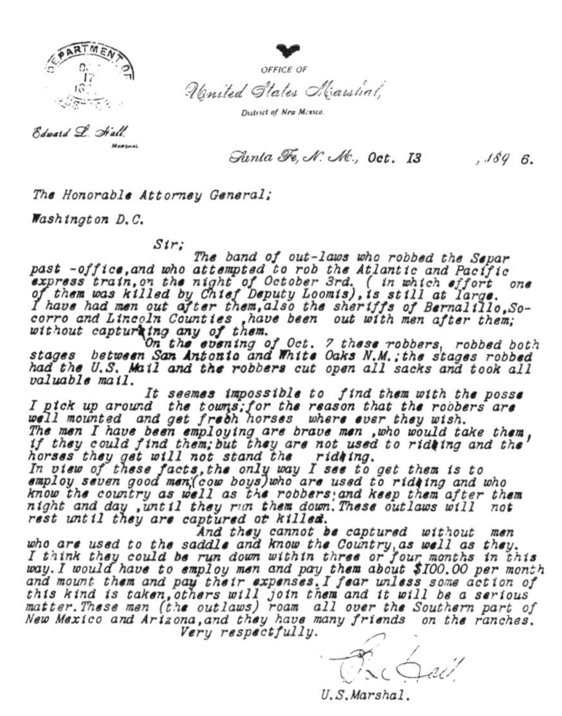

OFFICE OF
United States Marshal,
District of New Mexico.

Edward L. Hall
Marshal

Santa Fe, N. M., Oct. 13, 1896.

The Honorable Attorney General;

Washington D.C.

Sir;
The band of out-laws who robbed the Separ past -office,and who attempted to rob the Atlantic and Pacific express train,on the night of October 3rd. (in which effort one of them was killed by Chief Deputy Loomis),is still at large. I have had men out after them,also the sheriffs of Bernalillo,Socorro and Lincoln Counties ,have been out with men after them; without capturing any of them.

On the evening of Oct. 7 these robbers, robbed both stages between San Antonio and White Oaks N.M.;the stages robbed had the U.S. Mail and the robbers cut open all sacks and took all valuable mail.

It seemes impossible to find them with the posse I pick up around the towns;for the reason that the robbers are well mounted and get fresh horses where ever they wish. The men I have been employing are brave men ,who would take them, if they could find them;but they are not used to riding and the horses they get will not stand the riding. In view of these facts,the only way I see to get them is to employ seven good men,(cow boys)who are used to riding and who know the country as well as the robbers;and keep them after them night and day ,until they run them down. These outlaws will not rest until they are captured or killed.

And they cannot be captured without men who are used to the saddle and know the Country,as well as they. I think they could be run down within three or four months in this way. I would have to employ men and pay them about $100.00 per month and mount them and pay their expenses. I fear unless some action of this kind is taken,others will join them and it will be a serious matter. These men (the outlaws) roam all over the Southern part of New Mexico and Arizona,and they have many friends on the ranches.

Very respectfully.

E. L. Hall
U.S.Marshal.

A U.S. marshal writes to the attorney general in Washington in 1896 about the difficulties in apprehending the Black Jack bandits.
(National Archives, RG 60, Year Files)

There's not much of Ingalls, Oklahoma, today—the railroad was rerouted, highways bypassed the place, people moved on. The O.K. Hotel, the Ransom Saloon—all gone. A monument erected by citizens of Ingalls in 1938 to the three marshals who died there in 1893 was damaged when a trucker crashed into it. In late 1914, some old Oklahoma lawmen organized a company to make a film titled *The Passing of the Oklahoma Outlaws.* The lawmen included big names: Evett Nix, Chris Madsen, and Bill Tilghman. Tilghman was director. Back in Chicago, a kid named Lester Gillis was now six years old and about ready to see some movies.

6

DEALING OUT BLACK JACK

The law didn't look like much in Clifton, Arizona. The Clifton jail, built about 1881.

(National Archives, 111-SC-89496)

Magdelena, New Mexico
October 3, 1896
E.L. Hall, U.S. Marshal
Santa Fe, N.M.

Dear Sir:

At 7:45 last night the eastbound No 2 A. & P. regular passenger was just starting from the little Depot at the Rio Puerco—when a shot was fired and the air put on as heavily as to awaken my suspicions that we were held up. I went to front door of coach and stepped out right behind baggage car where about 20 or 30 shots up by the engine accompanied by swearing and loud talk removed all doubt as to what was up.

I ran back full length of coach to rear end where my shotgun lay with two buck shot shells in the magazine. I grabbed it and jumped off into the darkness and lay until I could get my eyes in shape to see after leaving the lights.

Then I could see a bunch of men about three car lengths ahead of me but knew they held some train men prisoners with them by the talk (It since turns out that they had the engineer only just then). So I dared not shoot at the bunch for fear of killing a train man—It was heavily clouded and so dark I could only barely distinguish a man's form. Pretty soon the man who was giving orders "to open the door"—"uncouple that" etc. stepped enough to one side to give me a chance.

I shot one load and he fell. He got up and fired sixshooter twice at me and I fired again. He disappeared. I could not then tell how but I know now that he simply rolled down the bank dead. That left me with no ammunition and some shells of bird shot in the train.

I returned to coach expecting them to follow me in but I think they did not fully realize that any one shot but their leader and did not see him fall down the bank.

I returned to the front trucks of the coach and the men meantime went forward and had the train pulled up a little. I caught on and jumped off when they slowed up and lit on the first tres-

tle of the bridge and fell about 4 feet into soft dirt and only slightly sprained my ankle.

Then they pulled up across the bridge and I swung on and went with them and got out by the tracks again. Could not kill another without risk of killing a railroader or express man as there were several people up in front.

Was in immediate danger from men behind on the train who happened to have pistols. They not knowing me from a robber.

They called "Cole," "Cole" and getting no answer they took to the tall weeds and left. I had the train let me get off just a little farther and crawled back to Cole's body and lay in the weeds waiting for them to come and hunt him. I could hear voices off some distance once but they never came back. I lay out there until 11:30 when a caboose with Hubbell, Farwolf and others and four saddle horses in a stock car came. Then left Hubbell and posse to take tail at daylight and went to Albuq. to take train here to try to head them off. Heard of saddle horses left by them near here and will go there to try to head them off.

Yours,

H. W. Loomis, Deputy

Horace W. Loomis, Chief Deputy, United States Marshal, District of New Mexico, was on his way to testify in a court case in Gallup, New Mexico, when the Arizona and Pacific train stopped in Rio Puerco, about forty miles west of Albuquerque. His report to his superior, Edward L. Hall, United States Marshal, concerned the Black Jack gang, a group of lads who, for primitive viciousness and mindless daring, had few equals.

THE LAW IN ARIZONA

ABOVE: Orient Saloon at Bisbee, Arizona, with a faro game in full blast, circa 1900.

(National Archives, 111-SC-93344)

ABOVE RIGHT: Early Arizona lawmen.

(Arizona Historical Society/Tucson, Port: Childress-Iles f. 7)

RIGHT: Arizona Rangers.

(Arizona Historical Society/Tucson, Winn F. Photo, folder 2)

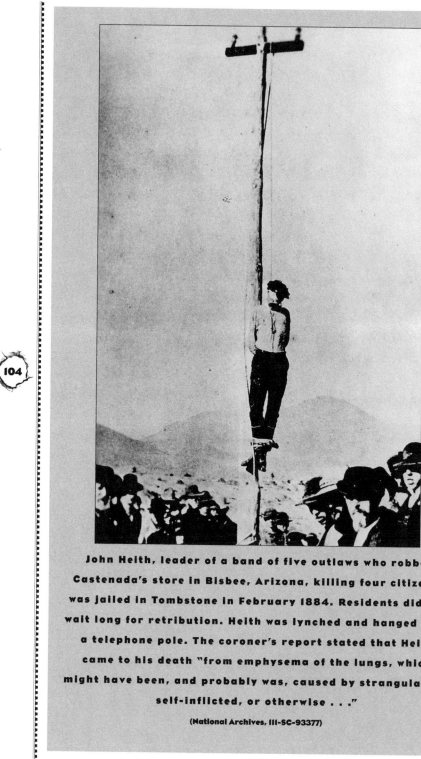

John Heith, leader of a band of five outlaws who robbed Castenada's store in Bisbee, Arizona, killing four citizens, was jailed in Tombstone in February 1884. Residents did not wait long for retribution. Heith was lynched and hanged from a telephone pole. The coroner's report stated that Heith came to his death "from emphysema of the lungs, which might have been, and probably was, caused by strangulation, self-inflicted, or otherwise . . ."

(National Archives, 111-SC-93377)

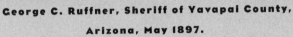

George C. Ruffner, Sheriff of Yavapai County, Arizona, May 1897.

(Arizona Historical Society, Port: Ruffner, George C. 42021)

In New Mexico, train robbing was, at least on the books, a crime punishable by death. Especially in the case of the Black Jack boys, this did not act as a deterrent. From 1896 to 1899, the gang held up numerous trains. They also robbed banks and post offices; they killed lawmen and citizens. They did not discriminate.

William "Black Jack" Christian did not give the gang his last name, opting, instead, for his nickname, which seemed better suited to the organization's pursuits. So he called it the Black Jack gang—"the Christian gang" would have seemed inappropriate. Christian had arrived in Arizona from Oklahoma in late 1895; he had been arrested several times in Indian Territory for robbing post offices and stores. In 1896 he began to organize his gang. Black Jack's friends included other monickered men—William Raper, alias William Walters, alias "Bronco Bill"; William "Kid" Thompson; and "Red" Pitkin. Cole Young, alias Cole Estes, was also among the upper echelon of the gang. In the spring of 1896, the Black Jack gang began its depredations. Cole Young met his end at the hands of Deputy Loomis several months later. In Young's case, bank robbing on that day turned out to be an offense punishable by death.

In August 1896, the gang had robbed a post office and Loomis had futilely led a posse across the desert, only to be outridden and outfoxed. Black Jack and his fraternity knew the country, had excellent horses and no hesitation to ride them nearly to death. The posses assembled by marshals were usually underpaid, underhorsed, and comprised of middling riders. At Rio Puerco, Loomis had unexpectedly come in contact with the gang and he had managed to take one of them out. But, in most instances, the deputy and his fellow lawmen were no match for the outlaws.

After the Rio Puerco incident, Loomis was on the trail again with another posse. Once again, he was outridden. Marshal Hall, burdened with attempting to restore some kind of order to New Mexico and thoroughly frustrated with the job, wrote to his employer, the United States attorney general in Washington, that Black Jack and his marauders were nearly impossible to catch. Their riding skills were too good, their horses too swift, their knowledge of the territory too extensive. And, like Jesse James, the outlaw band seemed to have friends everywhere. All over southern New Mexico and Arizona the band found allies among the thinly scattered cattle ranches, folks who provided food, weapons, and shelter. Whether they had cultivated such allegiance through deeds of friendship or through threats of bodily harm was unclear to the marshal. But another law enforcement official wrote that the ranchers had no choice: "Some of the owners are in sympathy with the outlaws and the news of a visit of a posse to their ranches could be scattered far and wide as fast as horseflesh could carry it. Even were the proprietors of all these ranches favorably disposed, they dare not sell or give aid to the posses. If they do so their lives and property would pay the penalty as has happened in the past."

Through their insolence and their skills, the Black Jack gang achieved one measure of respectability they didn't need; they united their pursuers. Sheriffs of several counties in Arizona and New Mexico decided to join forces with deputy marshals, Wells Fargo company men, other detective agency personnel, and forty Mexican soldiers whose assistance was secured through diplomatic channels.

Despite the growing force arrayed against them, Black Jack and friends looted stages between San Antonio and White Oaks, New Mexico, helping themselves to U.S. mail sacks containing all sorts of valuables. They robbed a group of cowboys camped on the range; robbed a Southern Pacific train near Separ, New Mexico; robbed a post office in San Simeon, Arizona, along with a store, a railroad office, and a bank. On March 28, 1897, the attorney general's office in Washington received the following telegram: "Necessary for safety of this vicinity that Black Jack and Gang be exterminated. . . . The Bank of Deming."

For periods of time the outlaws dispersed into Arizona, New Mexico, and south of the border and then reunited to plan new ventures. At times, they headquartered in the mountains in southeastern Arizona. On April 28, 1897, one of several posses recruited by the federal marshals managed to catch up with the outlaw band near Clifton, Arizona, and in the fighting made the big hit; Black Jack expired. Edward Hall, United States Marshal of New Mexico, was ecstatic, reporting to Washington that the killing of the despicable leader was the beginning of the demise of the entire gang.

It was not. Into the breach of outlaw leadership stepped one Tom Ketchum. A native of San Saba County, Texas, son of a doctor and youngest of three brothers, an uneducated ex-cowboy who had lived most of his days in New Mexico, Tom Ketchum had become fiercely loyal to the Black Jack legend, had reveled in the camaraderie of many of the Black Jack band with whom he had ridden, had become convinced that Black Jack should not die. Tom Ketchum thus decided to become the new Black Jack and assumed unto himself the mantle of authority.

Tom Ketchum and his brother Sam had always seemed a bit maladjusted, even in their own socially dysfunctional circles. One story that followed Tom involved his reaction after reading a letter from a lover spurning the outlaw in favor of another. In front of several of his friends, Tom drew his pistol and began to beat himself over the head with it. Tiring of that whipping, he then pulled out a saddle rope and began lashing himself with the new weapon. After that demonstration, many of Black Jack's comrades kept their distance.

But "Black Jack" Ketchum, as emotionally disturbed as many believed, was able to recruit new malcontents from the cowboy ranks. He was also able to talk some of the members of a gang called the Wild Bunch to join him in some robberies, although talk around outlaw circles was that one of the gang's leaders, Butch Cassidy, found Ketchum weird, unworthy of trust, and personally wanted nothing to do with him.

Tom "Black Jack" Ketchum's gang robbed new banks and post offices, and the new Black Jack carried on the spirited tradition of his forebear. From Arizona Territory came the usual lament: the Black Jack gang, wrote Marshal William Griffith, was "composed of nine men of the most desperate character who have sworn not to be taken alive. They defy any effort on the part of the civil or Federal authorities to arrest them and have notified some of the best and most influential citizens living in eastern Arizona that they will kill them at the first opportunity."

Arizona needed reinforcements, veteran manchasers who could not be employed cheaply, men who would track the devils into the seemingly impregnable southeastern mountains of the territory and wipe them out. With unfavorable newspaper publicity beginning to surface, with the pleadings of law enforcement officials from both Arizona and New Mexico becoming more frequent and frantic, the Justice Department acceded: more money was forthcoming.

The southwestern marshals were ecstatic. Quickly assembling a much larger posse of veteran gunmen and experienced riders, Marshal Griffith chased the gang through the Arizona mountain passes and across stark, thinly populated desert stretches, finally losing them across the Mexico border into the state of Chihuahua and the Sierra Madre Mountains. Black Jack returned the pressure, darting back into Arizona and New Mexico with as many as eleven men, more men than any single posse assembled by his pursuers, to rob some more post offices and banks. Griffith teamed with the new marshal of New Mexico Territory, Creighton Foraker, and the two joined forces with Wells Fargo agents and other private detectives hired by the Southern Pacific Railroad. The forces on both sides grew larger.

In August 1898, an Arizona deputy named Jeff Milton and a posse of Wells Fargo agents dispatched by Arizona Marshal William Griffith managed to stay on the track of the outlaws for several weeks, living on very little food and avoiding detection by the outlaws and their cattlemen allies by traveling only at night. The posse's work was as close to a feat of stealth and daring as had ever been accomplished by lawmen in the southeastern Arizona mountains. The posse surprised the gang and the resulting shootout brought the death of "Kid" Thompson and the capture of "Bronco Bill" Raper and several others. At last, law enforcement officials in the Southwest could report a victory, and in September, Marshal Foraker of New Mexico predicted the imminent extermination of Black Jack Ketchum.

"Black Jack" Christian, head of a gang that operated around Tombstone, Arizona, and in New Mexico in the early 1890s. When he was killed by federal marshals near Clifton, Arizona, in 1897, Tom Ketchum took over the "Black Jack" name. (Arizona Historical Society/Tucson, Port: Christian, "Black Jack" #4930)

In the winter of 1898 and spring of 1899, Black Jack took his battered comrades across the border again to rest and reinforce, with only an occasional post office or train robbery to keep up their income and to fuel the determination of their enemies to eliminate them. In late July 1899, the gang's fortunes began to unravel. Along with Wild Bunch outlaws Elza Lay and Kid Curry, the gang robbed a Colorado and Southern train near Folsom, New Mexico, eighty miles south of Trinidad. After the gang split the $30,000 disgorged by the dynamited safe, they rode into Cimarron Canyon and camped at Turkey Creek.

Marshal Foraker of New Mexico organized a hunting party in Cimarron and tracked down several of the gang members, including Sam Ketchum. Although the outlaws killed two of the lawmen, they suffered major losses of their own. Elza Lay, shot twice, was captured at the V. H. Lusk Ranch in Eddy County and was sent to the state penitentiary, where he would stay for a long stretch. Badly wounded in the left arm, Sam Ketchum was captured a few days later and sent to prison in Santa Fe. He died of blood poisoning.

In August 1899, brother Black Jack undertook a dramatic feat of retaliation: he tried to rob a train single-handedly outside Trinidad, Colorado, a location where his gang had hit trains two times before. After stopping the train, he ordered the engineer and fireman to uncouple the express car.

Tom "Black Jack" Ketchum.

(National Archives, 111-SC-93360)

"Black Jack" Ketchum prepares for hanging in Clayton, New Mexico, 1901.

(National Archives, 111-SC-93358)

Standing alongside the engine, Ketchum was an open target for several of the train crew. The railway mail clerk, who tried to shoot down the outlaw, failed and was shot through the face for his efforts. But the train conductor found the target, hitting Jack in the arm. Stumbling away from the train, the outlaw disappeared in nearby brush and the train pulled off.

The next morning Marshal Foraker and a posse arrived at the scene and there was Black Jack, crumpled just off the track, waving his hat on the barrel of his gun, his arm a shattered mass. They took the outlaw to prison and amputated his arm.

The territorial officials of New Mexico, working in concert with Justice Department heads in Washington, debated how to proceed judicially with the infamous bandit. In New Mexico, a man could be hung for train robbery; federal law provided only for a jail sentence. Considering the terror he had caused the community, the embarrassment he had been to law enforcement officials, and the financial loss he had caused territorial governments, there was no sentiment to keep Black Jack Ketchum in jail. They tried him for violating New Mexico's law against train robbing.

Tom Ketchum, minus one of his arms, marched to the gallows on April 25, 1901, in Clayton, New Mexico, the first man to suffer the capital penalty for robbing a train in New Mexico. From his jail cell the gang leader had watched the erection of the scaffold while taunting the workmen about killing a man for robbing a train. Smugly joking with the executioners, Ketchum, according to one witness, yelled out when the hood was placed on his head, "I'll be in hell before you start breakfast, boys!"

The execution was not decorous. The executioners overestimated the length of the drop necessary to kill the condemned, and, when the trap was sprung, Black Jack plummeted downward and downward, stopping only a short distance from the ground. The resulting sight was gruesome even for those spectators who normally found enjoyment in such proceedings. Black Jack's head spun violently apart from his body and rolled a few feet away.

Unlike Jesse James and Butch Cassidy and John Dillinger and other bandit legends who, with the aid of writers and researchers, will not stay dead in that house in Missouri or in

A hooded "Black Jack" being fitted with a rope on the gallows.

(National Archives, 111-SC-93359)

that small town in Bolivia or on that sidewalk in Chicago, no one ever claimed that Black Jack Ketchum survived his beheading. But, as with all noted figures in America's outlaw gallery, Black Jack inspired folk stories that lasted generations.

In 1936, shortly after the killing of John Dillinger in Chicago, western writer Roscue Logue authored *Tumbleweeds and Barb Wire Fences.* In telling the story of Black Jack Ketchum, Logue claimed that the outlaw, while awaiting execution, attempted to break out of prison using a pistol carved out of wood. Logue wrote, "While there he set an example for John Dillinger by carving a wooden pistol and wrapping it in tin-foil to resemble a silver mounted weapon." Years later, Ramon F. Adams, western historian and debunker of myths, quipped, "What we would like to know is how he [Black Jack] could carve a pistol with one hand."

Searching for Butch and Sundance

Butch Cassidy (seated, far right) and other Wild Bunch gang members. (National Portrait Gallery, NPC. 82.66)

BUTCH CASSIDY AND THE SUNDANCE KID, THEORY ONE: IN EARLY 1901 THE SUNDANCE KID (HARRY ALONZO LONGABAUGH), ACCOMPANIED BY A WOMAN NAMED ETTA PLACE, LEAVES NEW YORK CITY ON A STEAMSHIP. MONTHS later, after traveling to various locations, they arrive in Buenos Aires, Argentina. The following year, they are joined by Sundance's Wild Bunch gang partner, Butch Cassidy (Robert Leroy Parker). For a while the three live peacefully in the southern Patagonia region of Argentina and purchase a ranch. In February 1905, Butch and Sundance rob the Banco de Loudres y Tarapaca at Rio Gallegos of about $300,000. On December 5, 1905, joined by another Wild Bunch bandit, the gang robs another Argentina bank and flees to Chile and then to Bolivia. Three years later, in November 1908, Butch and Sundance heist a monthly payroll shipment being transported by mule from the Aramayo, Francke & Company tin and silver mines. They net about $90,000 but also attract to their trail a regiment of Bolivian soldiers. At a town called San Vicente, Butch and Sundance, trapped and wounded by Bolivian police, die by their own hands, and their bodies are buried together. The fate of Etta Place remains a mystery.

BUTCH CASSIDY AND THE SUNDANCE KID, THEORY TWO: In early 1901, the Sundance Kid, accompanied by Etta Place, leaves New York City on a steamship. Months later, after traveling to various locations, they arrive in Buenos Aires. The following year, they are joined by Sundance's Wild Bunch gang partner, Butch Cassidy. For a while the three live peacefully in the southern Patagonia region of Argentina and purchase a ranch. In February 1905, Butch and Sundance, accompanied by another Wild Bunch outlaw, rob the Banco de Loudres y Tarapaca at Rio Gallegos. In early 1908, Butch and Sundance stop a train near La Paz, Bolivia. During the robbery, a detachment of Bolivian cavalry attack the gang and Sundance is killed. In the last few minutes before he dies, he tells Butch that he and Etta were actually husband and wife. Cassidy escapes, sails to England, and then returns to the United States. In November 1908, two bandits are killed in a shootout in San Vicente, Bolivia. They are not Butch and Sundance but other Americans. Butch uses the publicity to lend credibility to the belief that he has been killed. He thus buries his outlaw past, moves to a little farm community in Michigan, and, under the name of William Phillips, marries a woman named Gertrude Livesay. The two settle in Globe, Arizona, and later in the state of Washington. Butch dies in 1937. The fate of Etta Place remains a mystery.

BUTCH CASSIDY AND THE SUNDANCE KID, THEORY THREE: In early 1901, the Sundance Kid, accompanied by Etta Place, leaves New York City on a steamship. Months later, after traveling to various locations, they arrive in Buenos Aires. The following year they are joined by Sundance's Wild Bunch gang partner, Butch Cassidy. For a while, the three live peacefully in the southern Patagonia region of Argentina and purchase a ranch. In March 1906, they rob the Banco de Nacion, at Villa Mercedes, San Luis. Tracked by Pinkerton agents sent to South America, the three travel to Bolivia. Among the various jobs the boys take in Bolivia to disguise their bandit identities is one at the Concordia Tin Mines southeast of La Paz, run by manager Percy Seibert, a close friend of Cassidy. In 1908 Seibert concocts a story that he feeds to Pinkertons and others about a shootout in San Vicente in which both Butch and Sundance perish. Butch and Sundance leave South America to start new lives in the United States. Butch, working as a guard in a mine in Nevada, is killed in 1941 in an accident. The Sundance Kid dies in Salt Lake City in 1955 under the alias of Hiram Beebe. The fate of Etta Place remains a mystery.

* * * * * * *

On the trail of Butch and Sundance. For some researchers it has meant many years of dogged, impassioned work—interviews with descendants; trips to remote areas of South America; correspondence with individuals in several countries; countless hours turning aging manuscript pages in archives, museums, libraries, courthouses, and penitentiaries; checking and rechecking leads. As they sift new evidence, the researchers sometimes change the contours of the theories, but the basic endings remain the same.

After all, how many different endings can a legend have? Butch and Sundance both die; Butch lives and Sundance dies; Butch and Sundance both live. No one, apparently, has suggested that Butch died and Sundance lived.

The research has taken on the aspect of the most modern, sophisticated, technological criminal investigation. In a crowded cemetery in San Vicente, high in the Andes mountains where winds incessantly whip dry brush against the markers, a research team of historians, Daniel Buck and Anne Meadows, and a forensic anthropologist, Clyde Snow, arrived in December 1991 to remove the bones of two men, purportedly gringo outlaws buried there over eight decades earlier. After negotiating with local officials, the team received permission to take some of the bones to the United States for forensic reconstruction and tests to compare the DNA component in the bones with the DNA of a known distant relative of Sundance. The research team concluded that the two men were definitely Anglo, that they definitely died of multiple gunshot wounds, and that they were not Butch and Sundance. The researchers now believe that they had been led to the wrong gravesite in the San Vicente cemetery. They believe that the bones of Butch and Sundance are in the ground in another grave in that cemetery. The research will continue.

In 1969, Twentieth Century Fox released *Butch Cassidy and the Sundance Kid,* a film produced by John Foreman and directed by George Roy Hill, starring Paul Newman as Butch, Robert Redford as Sundance, and Katherine Ross as Etta. Superbly written and shot, the film rocketed Redford's film career; it also rocketed the legend of Butch and Sundance into the forefront of western lore.

To movie fans in 1969, Butch Cassidy became the new Jesse James. Like Jesse, he was portrayed as a man of the people, at war against the oppressors of the common folk—in Jesse's case, Yankee rulers; in Butch's case, the moneyed railroad barons. Cassidy's own criminal career actually lasted longer than Jesse's—nineteen years compared to fifteen. Cassidy robbed banks and railroads and mine payroll shipments across the western United States and in South American countries. And he accomplished all of this with little personal violence.

But Butch Cassidy didn't have Jesse James's media representatives. He didn't have Major John Newman Edwards filling newspaper columns with worshipful essays extolling his exploits, didn't have dime novelists turning his life into the stuff of gallant warriors. He didn't have this until 1969.

The film followed the basic story line about Butch and Sundance that had been told and retold since 1930, when the western poet Arthur Chapman published an article in *Elks Magazine* titled "Butch Cassidy." The film included some of Chapman's story, with additional material furnished by other writers, and a different ending.

Through all of the telling and retelling, the relatively consistent part of the Butch Cassidy, Wild Bunch story has been

"THE WEST OF BUTCH CASSIDY."

About halfway between Casper and Buffalo, Wyoming, is "Hole-in-the-Wall," a gap washed through the wall of Red Canyon by a fork of the Powder River. It was here in the Red Wall country that such outlaws as Butch Cassidy rode this trail to a nearly impenetrable mountain stronghold.

(American Heritage Center, University of Wyoming, copyright restricted.)

ABOVE LEFT: Wooden jail in Wyoming Territory, 1893.

(National Archives, 22-WB-886)

LEFT: Saloons in Haven, Nevada, 1905.

(National Archives, 115-JQ-390)

The West of Butch Cassidy. "East on Main Street, Deadwood, Montana, 1877." (Montana Historical Society)

Saloon, Cheyenne, Wyoming, circa 1890s

(Wyoming State Museum, neg. 13095)

Butch's bank-robbing career in the United States. In remote Diamond Mountain in western Johnson County, Wyoming, a hideout known as "Hole-in-the-Wall" shielded a small army of thieves and desperadoes, men such as Harvey Logan (Kid Curry), Bill Carver, Ben Kilpatrick (The Tall Texan), Deaf Charley Hanks, Harry Tracy, Bob Meeks, Elza Lay, and the Sundance Kid, men who for several years thrived in the business of rustling cattle and robbing sheep camps, coal company paymasters, country stores, post offices, trains, and banks.

But the most celebrated of those who rode through the narrow passageway in the high, red sandstone ridge, those who became known as "the Wild Bunch," was Butch Cassidy. Son of a Mormon ranch family in the Sevier River country of central Utah, he became an expert horseman and pistoleer. His skills, along with his charismatic manner, gave Butch all the tools to rob and rustle with the best of them. He always had the quick joke, the smooth move in the most pressing situations. In and out of prison, he gained a reputation as resourceful, methodical, and cunning. He was a leader, a man who, many believed, preyed only on big moneyed livestock corporations and other rich interests who had bought up and controlled much of the West.

Employing the hit-and-run tactics of the guerrilla fighter, he outwitted and outran all the usual authorities on the hunt—sheriffs, marshals, Pinkertons, bounty hunters, and other police hired by railroads, banks, and cattle barons. His robberies usually featured a simple method—men to manage the horses, to handle the guns, and to fire the dynamite charges; and one man to handle the money. For getaways, Cassidy established relay stations at approximately fifteen-mile intervals for fresh horses, a kind of pony express system. Often, the escapes involved traveling over barren western hills and sand for a hundred miles or more. He used swift horses for the initial escape from the robbery scene and heavier thoroughbreds for the later endurance legs of the trip. A Wyoming federal marshal, frustrated with chasing the

Robert Leroy Parker (Butch Cassidy), circa 1883—
a cowboy before the Wild Bunch days.
(The Denver Public Library, Western History Department)

Wild Bunch, wrote to his superiors at the Justice Department in Washington: "Owing to the character of the country surrounding their rendezvous which permits the escape of fugitives into sections where it is impossible to apprehend them, and to the system employed by these outlaws of having their friends notify them of the appearance of a United States officer in their part of the country, the ordinary means of effecting an arrest cannot be successfully employed against them."

If ordinary means couldn't get the job done, railroad officials, with the backing of federal marshals, decided that extraordinary means would be used. They hired the best gunslingers available in several states to join in a manhunt to exterminate Butch and the other Wild Bunch gang members, gunslingers such as Joe LaFors, an unrelenting, skilled tracker. With this kind of pressure on him, Cassidy decided to relocate, to leave the country. He joined his Wild Bunch friend, the Sundance Kid, an ebullient, cocksure fast gun, in South America.

It is here, when Butch leaves the country, that the story becomes a subject of dispute, becomes an area of research that has fueled the energies and talents of several writers. A few years later, according to Chapman and others, the American bandidos finally succumbed to overwhelming odds at San Vicente. Badly wounded inside an adobe house, surrounded by Bolivian cavalrymen, Butch ended their outlaw saga with a bullet to the head of Sundance and a last cartridge to his own brain.

A few newspapers and magazines reprinted Chapman's story. So did the western printer and writer Charles Kelly. But the Butch and Sundance story never achieved heroic proportions until the film. It follows the basic Chapman story (Theory One) except in the details of the bandits' demise. Chapman wrote about suicide; this was too much for the moviemakers. In the film, Butch and Sundance, wounded and out of ammunition, exchange quips, leap to their feet, and dash into the courtyard and into a crossfire. The last frame of the film becomes a still shot of the two, guns raised—still alive. "You're gonna die bloody," a local sheriff had told the boys back in the States, "and you can only choose where."

Kid Curry, Wild Bunch gang member, after his arrest in 1897.

(Union Pacific Railroad Museum)

Newman and Redford ignited a Butch and Sundance research re-

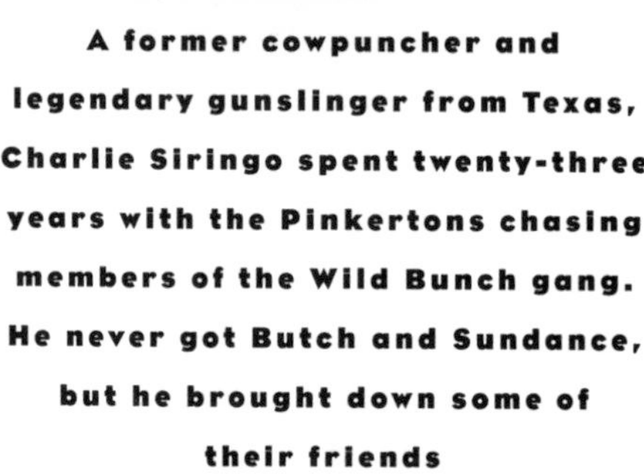

A former cowpuncher and legendary gunslinger from Texas, Charlie Siringo spent twenty-three years with the Pinkertons chasing members of the Wild Bunch gang. He never got Butch and Sundance, but he brought down some of their friends

(The Denver Public Library, Western History Department)

naissance. Who were these guys? Were the two outlaws as daring and charming as the movie suggested? Did they actually die at a shootout or were there other twists and contortions in the plot? Professional historians, western history buffs, and novelists embarked on a quest to find more on the alluring story. Unlike the myth of Jesse James, a story that began filling the pages of periodicals and dime novels almost before the events themselves unfolded, the Cassidy–Sundance Kid legend waited generations before making its impact. Now, such articles as "Butch, Sundance, Etta Place Frolicked in `Fun City'" and "Butch Cassidy Didn't Die in an Ambush in South America" and "Butch Cassidy in Patagonia" appeared in periodicals. Other stories in newspapers, historical society journals, and history magazines added to the store of information and theories. Larry Pointer, author of works on western history and rodeo history, concluded in his book *In Search of Butch Cassidy* that Butch survived Bolivia and lived out his life in Spokane, Washington (Theory Two). Carl Breihan, author of several influential books on the West, concluded that both the outlaws lived out long lives under aliases (Theory Three). Breihan's alias for Butch, incidentally, was not Pointer's alias. Both authors decided that Butch survived Bolivia; they argued as to the identity of the person Butch became. Breihan also concluded that Butch and Sundance were both involved romantically with Etta and that Butch had probably married her.

And so the work continues. More trips to South America. More research in documents. More interviews with descendants. Looking for another vital piece of information, another discovery that will lead further down the trail, the researchers carry on their work.

The legend, if not all of the facts, is established. Butch and Sundance, guns raised, still dash forward. Folks in Winnemucca, Nevada, have testified to that. On the morning of September 19, 1900, members of the Wild Bunch gang struck the First National Bank for three bags of gold coins reportedly worth over $32,000. As the bandits rode off, Deputy Sheriff George Rose climbed to the top of a nearby windmill in order to track the direction of the outlaws' escape. From

The formidable posse that trailed the Wild Bunch waits outside a train car to surprise its prey. (Pinkerton's Incorporated)

Butch Cassidy's train robberies were usually violent affairs, marked by dynamite explosions. This wrecked car was left near Wilcox, Wyoming. (Union Pacific Railroad Museum)

his vantage point high above Winnemucca, Sheriff Rose noticed a switch engine standing on a siding of a rail line that ran almost parallel to the road taken by the gang. Rose mobilized his posse, commandeered the locomotive, and roared after Butch Cassidy and his men. The train quickly closed the gap and the lawmen began firing at the fleeing outlaws as they crossed a wooden bridge over White's Creek. At the bridge, one of the outlaws dropped one of the sacks of money. The sheriff jumped off his horse, snatched up the sack, and rode off.

In nearby Clover Canyon, the posse nearly caught the outlaw band again. But Butch had planned ahead. Veering away from the tracks, he led his men to a camp where he had arranged for fresh horses. Changing mounts, changing directions, the Wild Bunch boys soon lost their pursuers.

Later in the year, following the prearranged script, they met in Texas. In Fort Worth, Butch purchased a bicycle and learned to perform circus tricks on it. The boys bought some expensive new clothes and some dapper bowlers, marched

The Sundance Kid and Etta Place pose in a photograph studio in New York in 1901, shortly before their departure for South America. (Pinkerton's Incorporated)

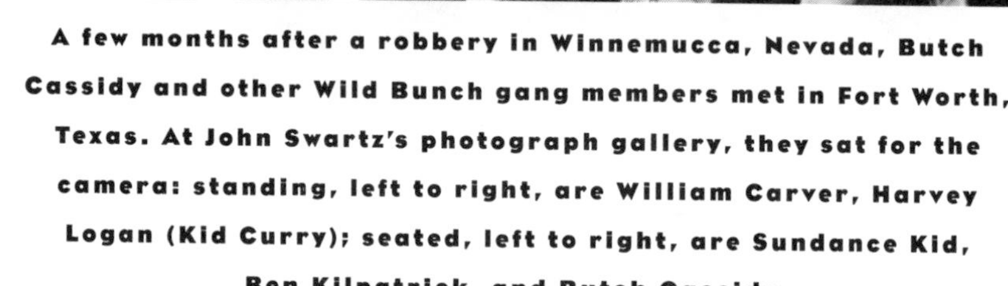

A few months after a robbery in Winnemucca, Nevada, Butch Cassidy and other Wild Bunch gang members met in Fort Worth, Texas. At John Swartz's photograph gallery, they sat for the camera: standing, left to right, are William Carver, Harvey Logan (Kid Curry); seated, left to right, are Sundance Kid, Ben Kilpatrick, and Butch Cassidy.

(National Portrait Gallery, NPG. 82.66)

over to Swartz's photograph gallery, and sat for a portrait—Sundance Kid on the left, Carver, the Tall Texan, Curry, and Butch. As soon as the photograph was developed, Butch mailed a copy back to the First National Bank in Winnemucca, thanking the bankers for their help in turning the Wild Bunch into a group of resplendent dressers. Today, the photo still hangs in a bank, the successor to the one the Wild Bunch robbed in 1900. For a number of years, citizens in Winnemucca celebrated Butch Cassidy Day, complete with softball games, barbecues, a parade, and a reenactment of the holdup. The legend prospered.

Bill Miner, circa 1906.

(Pinkerton's Incorporated)

THE FILM *THE GREY FOX* OPENS TO THE ROLLICKING SOUNDS AND SEPIA-TONED IMAGES OF A STAGECOACH ROLLING ACROSS THE DESERT FLOOR. FOUR ARMED BANDITS ON HORSEBACK, MOVING TO THE ACCELERATED MOTIONS OF EARLY MOTION-picture film, surround the stage and pull off a robbery in a matter of seconds.

Quick scene shift to an elderly man, with gray mustache, being released by a prison guard to the outside world.

The scene shifts again, this time in full color, to a turn-of-the-century railroad car. The aging gentleman, now in a broad-brimmed hat, suit, and tie, sits across from another gentleman, a salesman, who is extolling the great technological changes now sweeping the land. He speaks of the electrification of the American kitchen, from toasters and stoves that heat up all by themselves to other innovations such as an apple-peeling device, which he proudly produces from his bag. The older man is fascinated about the talk of progress. After a few minutes the salesman asks of the older man what line of work he is in. The man replies that he is presently between jobs. And what profession is he in? "I rob stagecoaches."

❋ ❋ ❋ ❋ ❋ ❋ ❋

William (Bill) Miner, alias

George Edwards, alias Bill Morgan, alias John Luck, alias George Budd, alias California Bill; later known as "Old Bill Miner." Much later, in movie fiction, known as the Grey Fox. Most bandit folk heroes led meteoric, violent lives. They lived for the thrill of the escape, for the chance to carry out the daring deed, to utter the memorable quip, or to make the great hit. In that kind of quest, they took grievous risks. Jesse, most of the Daltons, Sam Bass, Black Jack Ketchum—their careers and their lives were relatively short; their line of work drove down the life expectancy average.

But one of the Old West outlaws, Bill Miner, did manage to survive, even thrive, into old age. Even though over thirty of those years were in residence in San Quentin, where his odds for staying alive increased, Miner's recorded outlaw deeds nearly spanned the generations from Jesse to John Dillinger. He was genial, mannered, a story-telling character who made eager newspaper reporters salivate for a story. He talked about robbing only corporations and injuring only the industry barons who made the lives of most Americans more difficult. He talked about giving stolen loot to the poor. He talked about great stage-robbing and train-robbing stunts and about his own place in bandit history. Inspiring headlines not only in the United States but in Canada, he made friends in various walks of life, from businessmen to reporters, even to law enforcement officials. On one occasion, when he was returned to prison after a grueling escape attempt through Georgia swamp waters, crowds gathered to cheer his efforts and even threw money and cigars at him. He doffed his hat, returned to his cell, and continued to write his autobiography.

Although a seasoned criminal, Bill was justifiably seen as less threatening than other bandit types, shunning violence in favor of subterfuge and guile, qualities that, unfortunately for him, were often more elusive than real. All those years in prison testify to his lack of outlaw wizardry. Yet, banditry for Bill Miner was not a series of foolhardy acts of brazenness that could get him killed but a way of life filled with subtle refinements. He lived to enjoy the notoriety, to play mind games with his listeners, to spin tales for which he gave little or no hard evidence. Take what you believe from his story-telling repertoire, you fellow outlaws, you writers, you historians, you newspaper reporters; he was there to offer a grand dose.

Like Jesse and the Youngers, he began his criminal career in the Civil War years, stealing horses and robbing stagecoaches. In December 1865, about the same time Bill Quantrill was killed in Kentucky, Miner stole several hundred dollars from a mining corporation; in 1911, years after the outlaw deeds of Butch Cassidy and the Sundance Kid and the Wild Bunch had ended, nearly thirty years after Jesse had been killed, Bill robbed a Southern Railway Express in Georgia. He was taken to jail in an automobile.

He was born near Onondaga, in Ingham County, Michigan, in 1846. Following the death of his father, Miner's mother took the family to California, settling in a rich gold-mining town in Placer County called Yankee Jims. In 1864, at age eighteen, Bill joined up with the Union Army in the California Cavalry Volunteers. Rebelling against the military discipline of his unit, he deserted after only three months.

He returned to Yankee Jims and for a time worked the mines, hoping for the big find. When the restless youngster didn't strike it big in the mines, it inspired his hatred of the big mining companies and of corporate structures, of a system that paid off owners in riches and paid off the workers with part-time work, squalid housing, and slave wages. Bill Miner deserted again.

He was now, he said, "on the rob." In December 1865, a day after his birthday, Miner stole a suit, a watch, and a horse. A few days later, teamed up now with a partner, he stole some more horses, sold them, and headed for the bars, brothels, and gambling halls of San Francisco.

In late January 1866, Miner and his accomplice were arrested in Woodbridge, California, for horse stealing and armed robbery and sent to San Quentin. During the trial, the judge in Stockton who oversaw the Miner case remembered the youngster as almost buoyant at the proceedings. It was as if the prison sentence was a badge of courage, the first honor accorded a fledgling outlaw. When Miner and his partner were taken aboard a steamer for the short ride to "The Stones," as San Quentin was fondly called by its inhabitants, the two prisoners stood on the deck waving handkerchiefs in the air as if they were off on a Mediterranean cruise. A reporter for a Stockton newspaper who witnessed the performance declared, "A more thorough evidence of perverted nature we never saw."

His first stay at San Quentin, the place that would become home for much of his life, lasted for a little more than four years, and his contact with various robbers, thieves, con men, and murderers convinced him that his previous criminal life lacked focus. Stealing horses, sometimes one at a time; holding up individuals for pocket cash; and pilfering suits—for God's sake, this was not an auspicious career beginning. Bill decided to burgle homes and to rob stagecoaches.

His partner was Alkali Jim Harrington, veteran burglar and stage robber, a man who was serving his third term at San Quentin when Bill made his acquaintance. In January 1871, the duo hit a few homes in San Jose, robbed a stage near Angels Camp and another near San Andreas. By June the two were back in San Quentin.

Bright, sensitive, a man with both a sense of humor and a feeling for the dramatic, Miner became a San Quentin legend by the time he was in his thirties, and his life a succession of attempted jailbreaks, some successful; trials; appeals; releases; new partners; new robberies; tall tales; newspaper clippings; near escapes from a violent end; and the expenditure of extraordinary energies in devising plots and schemes, most of which failed. In October 1880, after a successful stage robbery in Colorado, Miner bought two trunkloads of clothes and headed back to Michigan, back to his birthplace, Onondaga. The Sherman House, best hotel in town, now became the temporary residence of a rising financial baron, William A. Morgan.

William Pinkerton, the oldest son of Allan, founder of Pinkerton's, sits at his desk surrounded by memorabilia of the family business. Unlike other lawmen, Pinkerton never underestimated the guile and ingenuity of Bill Miner.

(Library of Congress, LC-USZ62-50013)

Perhaps he should have been on the con all along rather than on the rob. Flitting about town in an elegant suit, twirling a cane, his manners of a most courteous and refined nature, the fictitious financier entranced the best citizens of Onondaga with stories of vast land deals, magnificent gold strikes in the California hills, and his own considerable fortune. Miner stayed in Michigan long enough to become engaged to the daughter of one of the town's most successful entrepreneurs. When his money ran out and the whole charade threatened to collapse around him, he claimed that his desperately ill mother needed him in California. After being feted at a banquet hosted by Onondaga's most prominent citizens, Miner left his hometown never to return.

By Christmas 1881, Miner was back in San Quentin, this time for robbing a stage in California near Sonora. After several aborted escape attempts from the Stones in the following years, Miner decided on a new tactic—he would resort to written persuasion. Between September 1897 and November 1898, he penned several letters to the governor of California, lamenting his previous folly in engaging in dishonest pursuits, promising to apply his natural talents to society's interest. The governor didn't buy it. It was not until June 17, 1901, that Bill Miner again walked out of San Quentin. He was fifty-four years old; he had spent over thirty-three of those years behind bars. But his longevity was making him legendary.

When Bill Miner walked out of San Quentin, he walked into the twentieth century. He was a man whose profession was robbing stagecoaches; time had made him an anachronism. There were few buffalo on the western plains; there were even fewer stagecoaches.

For a time he worked as an oyster picker near Whatcom, Washington, and lived with his sister and her husband. But oyster picking was a hopeless substitute for robbery. Thieving was the essence of the man, whatever his skills. The veteran ex-con was on the loose again and neither advancing age nor a lack of stagecoaches would hold him down. He turned to trains.

Hooking up with a former inmate at San Quentin and with a seventeen-year-old neophyte, Miner attempted to rob the Oregon Railway and Navigation Express at a spot about ten miles from Portland. He came outfitted with the proper equipment—red signals to persuade the engineer to stop and several sticks of dynamite to blow open the express car door. But when Miner sent one of the men to the track bed with the stop signals, none of the three men knew how to use them. When the train approached, the engineer saw a man frantically waving the signals on the wrong side of the tracks and ignored him. For Miner, this new profession offered new embarrassments. For a time, Bill went back to the oyster beds.

In 1902, Cowboy Jake Terry, a counterfeiter who had been one of Miner's cell mates at San Quentin, served out his most recent sentence and returned to his home state of Washington. The two renewed their friendship, and Bill Miner quickly returned to crime. Terry had once been a railroad engineer and knew Canadian rail routes. They headed north.

With Jake Terry as a partner, Miner, for the first time in his already relatively long life, became a successful thief. In September 1904, the two, accompanied by a third man, Shorty Dunn, hit the Canadian Pacific Railway's transcontinental express near Mission Junction, forty miles east of Vancouver. By tapping the telegraph wires, Miner and Terry had learned that a consignment of gold dust was being shipped to the United States assay office in Seattle. The gang made off with several thousand dollars in money and gold dust, $50,000 in United States bonds, and several hundred thousand dollars in Australian securities. They had pulled off a major success; they had also pulled off the first recorded train robbery in the history of Canada. Now, this was the stuff of legends!

Although the Australian securities and United States bonds were hot even for the most daring fences and thus of no immediate monetary value to Miner, the potential damage for the Canadian Pacific was considerable. Not only did the theft of the bonds pose a possible huge financial loss to the company, the incident itself threatened to be a public relations disaster. The railroad desperately wanted the bonds returned; Miner hid them for possible bargaining power sometime in the future.

In June 1905, the *New York Times* reported that the Canadian Pacific Railway had, through the cooperation of Jake Terry, recovered some of the securities. But Terry was dealing only with his portion of the loot; Bill Miner still had his own insurance.

Bill Miner, one of the last of the nineteenth-century bandit kings, never used a car. Ushering in a new generation, automobiles arrive at Fort D. A. Russell, Cheyenne, Wyoming, 1906.

(Wyoming State Museum, neg. 1789)

In early October 1905, Miner and Terry were still acting as a team, even after Terry's negotiations with the Canadian Pacific. The duo robbed a Great Northern Overland train near Seattle of an amount rumored to be more than $30,000.

With private investigating teams for both railroads now furiously on the hunt, with Canadian and U.S. authorities and Pinkertons and others cooperating in an unprecedented coordinated chase, Miner quietly settled on a ranch in British Columbia, spending his own Great Northern spoils in regular, managed amounts. He enjoyed riding, hunting, smoking his pipe, and chewing on his "poppy root"—opium pills. He worked on his memoirs. He talked about how he had traveled to Europe on a grand tour, how he had worked in the slave trade in Turkey, how he had run guns in Rio de Janeiro, and how he had hoodwinked Pinkertons (and sheriffs, and marshals, and European and South American authorities). Historians eighty years later would still accept his wild tales of international intrigue and bandit bravado as fact.

But Bill Miner was never content while outside prison walls to enjoy the freedom. There seemed to be in the man an almost primitive urge to rob, a kind of elemental need beyond his own financial condition, an obsession that could not be quieted even with money in hand. In May 1906, Bill again hit the Canadian Pacific, this time the Imperial Limited, near Ducks. The take: around $15 and some catarrh tablets. The old bandit not only hit a dud; he stirred to even greater action the British Columbia Provincial Police, who, with the help of Indian scouts and the Royal Northwest Mounted Police, rode after Miner through driving rain and over fields turning to mud. For the sake of Canadian law enforcement, for the sake of railroad interests, the Mounties and their allies charged after the elusive crook whose story had become a national embarrassment. Bill Miner had to be rounded up.

On May 14, 1906, they caught him. After five years on the run, Miner was back in custody. When the Mounties brought him into the town of Kamloops in a wagon, a large crowd had gathered in the rain to see the infamous bandit. The *Kamloops Standard* pictured Miner "with grizzled hair and moustache, erect and active," not appearing "to bear within the weight of age which the prison records now credit him with."

After a trial in which Bill was convicted and sentenced to life imprisonment at the penitentiary at New Westminster, British Columbia, enormous crowds again gathered to see him off. Some people handed him cigars. One of the residents summed up the feelings of many of the citizens: "Don't judge our friend too harshly." After all, Old Bill robbed from the rich and gave to the poor. Robin Hood. Jesse. Bill Miner.

At his trial, Bill made the kind of statement for which reporters covering bandit life have always offered hosannas.

"No prison walls can hold me," Miner declared gruffly. The man was a prophet. On August 8, 1907, the cagey con, even while suffering from sore feet, managed to escape through a tunnel he and other inmates had dug under a high-board prison fence. He eluded detectives; he eluded a special bloodhound brought in from Vancouver. Many residents told authorities that they didn't know where the old guy was—and that, if they did, they wouldn't rat on him anyway. One Vancouver resident said that many people considered him a magnificent throwback to the bandits of yore.

Bill Miner was never again in the clutches of Canadian authorities. Years later, evidence surfaced in the press about Bill's escape in 1907. It seems that in the weeks prior to the event, he had talked with several visitors at the prison, including detectives. It seems, also, that a number of police officials who inspected the tunnel under the fence were of the opinion that no human, especially an old man nursing a bad foot, could have crawled through. Could the escape have been an elaborate ruse? Could prison officials, acting on orders from the Canadian government authorities, have allowed Miner to walk in return for the securities he had hidden? Could the Canadian Pacific Railway have convinced Canadian officials to participate in such a plot?

After a series of charges and countercharges in the press and after contentious debate in the Canadian Parliament, the government decided that a full investigation was not appropriate. No official inquiry ever resolved the controversy. Bill Miner never admitted that he was at the center of a conspiracy by Canadian officials to recover the stolen bonds. Several ex-cons, investigative journalists, and historians have suggested, nevertheless, that old Bill did not crawl out of his imprisonment that day at New Westminster.

For the second time in his life, Miner took on the life of the rich dandy—fashionable clothes, diamond stickpins, culinary and sexual excesses; these were rewards for years of bandit labor. He returned to the United States and lived for a time in Denver. When his finances gave out in early 1910, Bill decided to come out of retirement. He would nab another train.

Perhaps the southern states, a new region where he had never before worked, would be vulnerable, he reasoned. Accompanied by two young recruits, he traveled to Georgia. The team robbed a train at White Sulphur Springs, netting a little more than $2,000. Stalked by private, state, and federal detectives and marshals, plagued by extremely cold weather, Bill was apprehended in a lodging house in early February 1911. He was sixty-four years old.

Newspapers across the country jumped on the story. With the headline "JESSE JAMES RIVAL AGAIN UNDER ARREST," the *Sacramento Daily Bee* reported: "'Old Bill' Miner, second only to Jesse James in notoriety as a train robber, was one of the White Sulpher, Ga., bandits arrested at Gainesville, Ga., last Thursday as asserted by the National Detective Agency here today." Miner was famous, the article declared, "as one of the 'bad men' of the Northwest." In Chicago, in Atlanta, in Canada, the news hit the papers that a relic of the Wild West was again in custody for robbing a train. They called him "fearless" and "defiant"; one called him an "old rooster." They talked about how he had charmed the audience at the trial, about how, after his conviction, he turned to some women in the gallery, swept his hat in a bullfighter's motion, and declared that when one breaks the law, one must pay the penalty and that the golden rule was still the best law to govern the country. One reporter said that the state of Georgia had never before seen such a spectacle of a legal case. With élan and charm, Miner played the legend to the hilt. One scribe said that Old Bill was more than simply garrulous; he would talk nonstop, spinning story after story. He could, said the reporter, "talk the arms off a billy goat." Jesse and Bill, Bill and Jesse; the first of the great outlaws; perhaps, newspapers concluded, the last of the great outlaws.

In March 1911, William Pinkerton, head of the national crime-busting agency, came to Georgia on business. "Bill Miner will get away; mark my words," he told a reporter. "That fellow's a fox, he is. You can't keep a man in a road

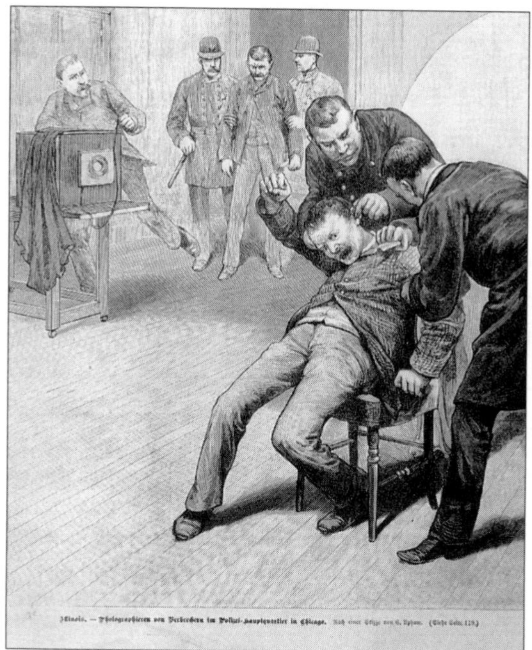

The new generation would bring new police methods. This wood engraving, "The Reluctant Model," depicts the beginnings of the mug shot. (National Portrait Gallery, NPC. 80.7)

camp who can get through brick walls." More ingredients to the legend. Bill Miner's escape record was even less impressive than his bank-robbing record; yet Pinkerton himself had bought into the reputation. The fox was still alive and still attempting to rob banks. The fox was a special bandit animal.

On March 15, Miner was sent to the Newton County Convict Camp to work on a chain gang. He told prison officials that he was ill, that his nerves were gone, and that he was "all in." He petitioned the Georgia State Prison Commission for a transfer to the new Milledgeville prison farm, a minimum security institution near Macon and the Oconee Forest, a place more suited to his age and condition. The public, reading of his plea in the newspapers, sent letters of support. In July, Miner received his transfer to the prison farm in Milledgeville; in October, he escaped. One newspaper wag reported: "Old Bill Miner Was 'All In,' Now Bill Miner Is 'All Out.'" The *Atlanta Constitution* questioned whether this was the age of young men. Consider Bill, the septuagenarian: "With the suppleness of a kitten and the guile of a serpent he is somewhere squirming his way through Georgia, enjoying

life . . . and quietly laughing in his sleeve at all the excitement he has kicked up."

William Pinkerton had been right, and the Southern Railway Company now called for his company's services. Eighteen days later Bill was back in jail. Crowds greeted his arrival in Milledgeville; newspapers talked about his politeness, his wit, and his age.

Seven months later, Miner again escaped. The problem at Milledgeville was not the escape from the facility; the problem was surviving the environment around it. For three days he wandered through the swamps trying to live on blackberries and bad water. When he visited a farmhouse twenty miles from the prison farm, he was again apprehended.

Back in Milledgeville, a large crowd again gathered to pay homage to the ancient warrior. They whooped and shouted and threw cigars. They filled a hat with money. Bill waved his appreciation.

This time there would be no more escapes. On September 2, 1913, Bill Miner died after a severe bout with gastritis. Before his death he told the warden stories of the old days. He talked about great deeds in Africa and Europe and about robbing only corporations. And he talked about Jesse James. He had ridden with Jesse, Bill claimed. In a way, he had.

❋ ❋ ❋ ❋ ❋ ❋ ❋

The film concludes. In handcuffs, Bill Miner, along with two compatriots, is led aboard a train headed for the British Columbia penitentiary. A caption then reveals that Miner on August 8, 1907, escaped, eluded an intensive manhunt, and was never seen in Canada again. Miner's lover, a woman named Kate Flynn, who had opened a photography studio in Chicago, is seen in Europe in the company of a wealthy mining engineer named George Anderson.

❋ ❋ ❋ ❋ ❋ ❋ ❋

Fade to last image: Bill Miner, dressed in prison stripes, runs to freedom.

9

MYTHMAKING

San Diego police
stand ready, 1911.
(Museum of San Diego History)

IN BALLADS AND ODES THE LEGENDS GREW—ABOUT MISUNDERSTOOD TRAILBLAZERS LAID OUT BY TREACHERY AND BAD FATE, ABOUT HEROIC BADMEN OF THE PLAINS HORSE STEALING, STAGE ROBBING, TRAIN ROBBING, AND BANK ROBBING, MOSTLY FOR honor and pride, not for money. In song, Cole Younger and Bill Quantrill became Robin Hoods. In song, so did Jesse:

Jesse James was a lad who killed many a man.
He robbed the Glendale train.
He stole from the rich and he gave to the poor,
He'd a hand and a heart and a brain.

In 1915, when officers asked train robber Frank Ryan why he had turned from a life of respectability to that of a thief, he answered, "Bad companions and dime novels. Jesse James was my favorite hero. I used to read about him at school when us kids swapped dime novels." To make a name like Jesse's or Butch's or some of the other outlaws'; to leave behind the life of anonymity; to grab some quick bucks—it was all there in the dime novels, in the stories and songs

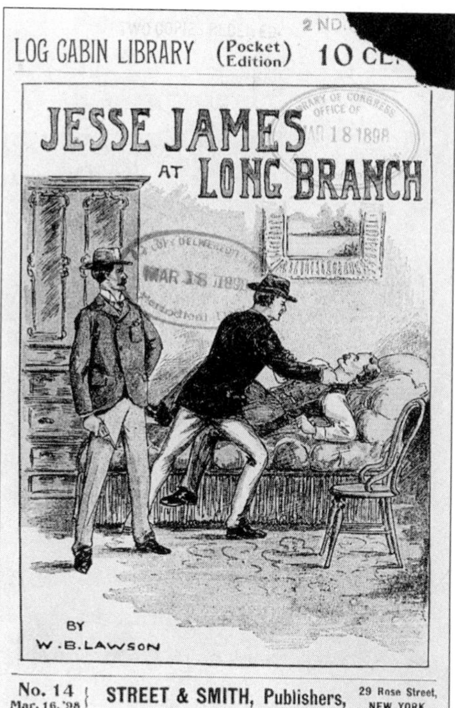

From dime novels such as these two Log Cabin Library productions Americans read about a legendary West, especially about Jesse James and the Youngers. (Library of Congress, PZ1L828, nos. 14 and 15)

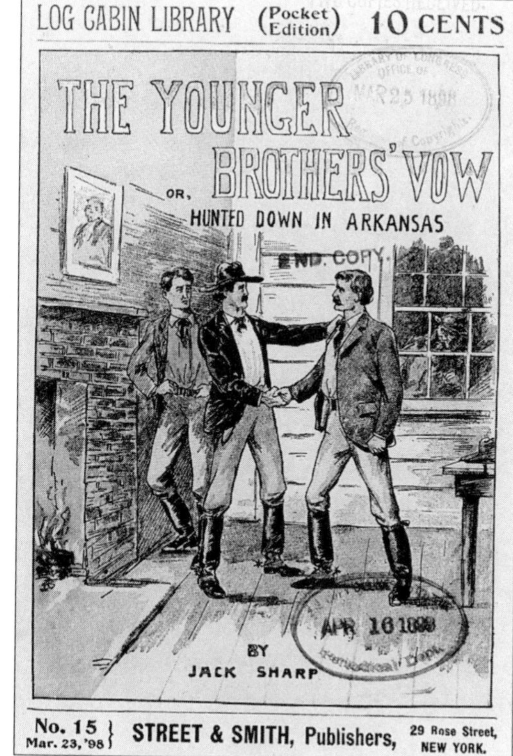

and poems handed down in the little dog-eared books.

The New York Detective Library presents *The James Boys in a Fix,* price—ten cents; Wide Awake Library presents *The James Boys' Bridges,* price—fifteen cents; Log Cabin Library presents *Jesse, the Outlaw: A Narrative of the James Boys by Capt. Jake Shackleford, the Western Detective,* price—ten cents. The dime novel—for kids and their parents in New York or Indianapolis or Columbus, the West was only a dime novel away; the West, where the mysterious forces of civilization and anarchy locked in a precarious battle. For a dime you could get Deadwood Dick, the Prince of the Road; the Red Revenger; Oonomoo the Huron; Billy the Kid; Buffalo Bill; Captain Crimson, the Man of the Iron Face; or Jesse James. It was here that fact and fiction melted into one great glob of pulp. It was here in America's cheap thriller industry that the western outlaw hero was first mass-produced.

In 1860 the New York publishing house of Beadle and Adams issued Anne Stephens's *Malaeska: The Indian Wife of the White Hunter.* Amid the economic dislocation and havoc of the war, the dime novels, published in various sizes and formats, with print runs sometimes reaching over 100,000, brought an escapist fare that survived as a popular form of literature for several decades. Other publishers—such as Street and Smith's, Richard Fox, and Frank Tousey—joined Beadle in a frantic production of cheap paper and ink and hack prose and a fierce competition for sensationalist tastes. In 1883, Tousey, whose graphic depictions of violence pandered even more than the others to those sensationalist tastes, was forced by the United States postmaster general to stop printing some of his outlaw titles under the threat of losing his second-class mailing privileges.

Although some of the pulp fiction heralded the adventures of pirates and warriors of foreign deserts, fully three quarters of the settings for the books were in the American frontier, the haunt of the backwoodsman, the cowboy, the plainsman, and the outlaw. Some early attention was accorded to a horse thief, gunslinger, jailbreaker, and murderer who called himself "Billy the Kid." The story of the Kid, according to one western reporter, was so distorted by the eastern press, susceptible to Billy's own self-promotion, that Americans "have about as good an idea of what Billy really was, as a burro has of the beauties of Milton."

In the years after his death at the hands of Pat Garrett in July 1881, the character of the Kid would appear in the movies with Dracula and Mickey Mouse and Jane Russell, would have parade floats depict his murder, would be the subject of short stories and plays and novels by such authors as Gore Vidal and Zane Grey, would be memorialized by Woody Guthrie, Bob Dylan, and Billy Joel, and would be the subject of a score composed by Aaron Copeland that later served as a waltz, a ballet, and a piano solo. The image of the infamous ruffian would swell and bloat after a frenzy of tall tales and misrepresentation. Billy the Kid became a vehicle for almost any kind of expression or theory or insight into the American West; his life itself was almost totally absorbed in a haze of fantasy.

The Kid has endured as a figure around whom literary, media, and entertainment craftsmen have woven a seemingly endless pattern of western tales. But the favorite of the early pulp writers was not Billy the Kid; it was Jesse, a man whose actual deeds and long career provided a framework for the bandit hero. In the case of Billy the Kid, the Robin Hood comparisons came much later, long after the events of his actual life ceased to matter. In the case of Jesse, many writers during his own lifetime portrayed him in an admiring light. He was endowed with romantic and respectable qualities, motivated by revenge for foul deeds committed against him and his people, and imbued with reckless courage. He was the preeminent outlaw hero.

By 1903, more than 270 stories about Jesse James had made the pages of the pulp industry. Some were loosely based on fact; others were totally imaginative. All were fanciful, based on stories passed down by imperfect memories, altered by conscious and unconscious exaggeration, and slanted by

ROBBERY OF THE EXPRESS CAR.

"Robbery of the Express Car"–this woodcut by Western Engineering Company illustrated an 1877 book on the history of crime.

(Library of Congress, LC-USZ62-39654)

temperament, motive, and literary skill. The story of Jesse, like the stories of other western heroes and badmen, is a terrain over which even the surefooted can stumble.

The western writer and bibliographer Ramon Adams, after a long career of examining books on the Wild West, declared in 1964, "Nowhere has research been so inadequate or writing so careless as in accounts of Western outlaws and gunmen." Adams became a kind of western writing muckraker, his mission to sift out the most ludicrous fabrications and inconsistencies in published histories of the West. After labo-

riously poring through more than eleven hundred books and pamphlets, he pronounced only about two dozen, a little more than two percent, to be "reliable." These two dozen included a few privately printed articles and some books published by university presses (yet even some among the two dozen, Adams said, had their own "minor" flaws). For the reader wishing to know the facts, then, Adams had only sympathy. The soil of western literature, the bibliographer demonstrated, was mostly sludge.

For Americans of all ages and in various parts of the country in the late nineteenth century, perceptions of the West were largely shaped by newspapers, magazines, and pulp novels. Images of the beauty and dangers of the wilderness, tales of the fortunes made by those who were lucky and resourceful, descriptions of the range of human characters inhabiting the untamed frontier—all of it was shaded in bits of information and perceptions. Reporters and writers saw in the western outlaw a mix of traits, from the gritty loner who faced hardship with rectitude and guts to the demon predator lurking in terrible hellholes of crime; from the reluctant thief and killer to the eager thief and killer; from the defier of odds and convention to the defiler of law and order.

Billy the Kid, Jesse, Sam Bass, the Daltons and Youngers, and the Hole-in-the-Wall bunch all embodied a combination of these conflicting strains of good and evil and assumptions about justice, a well-ordered society, freedom, and individual rights. None of the outlaws upon whom the writers lavished most of their attention were "all bad." There was some aspect of their past, some content in their characters, from which the authors could find redemptive features, from which heroic elements could be passed on. To characterize these men as driven by a complex web of emotion and motive was to separate them from senseless marauders and murdering thugs; was to create some sense of identification, some vicarious connection with the readers; was, most importantly, to sell more books.

As the first great generation of outlaw heroes passed into history and legend, as the retelling and remaking of these figures took on an independence apart from the lives themselves, American audiences would soon begin to see the West from a wholly new perspective. They would now experience, from a budding medium, the robberies, chases, escapes, and death about which they had only read.

In the summer of 1893, at the World's Columbian Exposition in Chicago, thousands of visitors squinted into something called the "peephole kinetoscope." Although several devices creating the illusion of movement had gained attention in the United States and abroad since early in the nineteenth century, Thomas Edison, from his production laboratories in East Orange, New Jersey, which he called "Black Maria," had perfected his kinetoscope to such a degree that commercial use now seemed possible. Edison was determined, he said, to "do for the eye what the phonograph does for the ear." He had brought commercial phonographs to the world; he was now bringing commercial motion pictures. Along with other entrepreneurs, he was also bringing a medium that would shape the image of the American West and the legends of the outlaw hero.

The early motion picture industry featured two markedly different delivery modes. Edison's device, designed for individual users, first appeared in a commercial parlor in New York City in April 1894. A year later, a company in New York introduced a primitive projecting machine that could entertain a room of viewers at the same time. They called it an "eidoloscope." On these machines, viewers for the first time

In the *National Police Gazette,* readers were treated to such images of the West as "Fierce Bandits at Bay," a confrontation of detectives and criminals in a Nebraska hotel dining room in 1882.

(Library of Congress, LC-USZ62-63907)

could see a gun battle, watch a gang on horseback rob a train, see a bank holdup. They could more vividly experience the sights of western landscape and the movement of western cowboys.

The last years of the century ushered in a flurry of technological improvements, from the Lumiere cinematographe to the phantascope. At a small theater at the Cotton States Exposition in Atlanta, Georgia, in October 1895, a company began to show films produced by Edison on a large screen. At vaudeville theaters such as Keith's in Boston and

A still from *The Great Train Robbery*, the first great movie depiction of the West.

(The Museum of Modern Art)

Philadelphia, Proctor's in New York, Hopkins in Chicago; at amusement parks such as Coney Island; at kinetoscope parlors such as Talley's in Los Angeles; and at playhouses, opera houses, and converted storefronts in several large cities, commercial cinema began to stir the American public.

In the early years, motion pictures were primarily vehicles for news and short features. But by 1902, the Edison Company was technologically able and financially equipped to produce large-scale "story films." Early in the century, many large urban centers had one or more "nickel theaters" or "nickelodeons," which featured programs that lasted from ten minutes to an hour. The Biograph Company, chief commercial rival of Edison, became the foremost producer of "story films" by 1904. The motion picture business was emerging as a form of mass entertainment.

In the darkness of the theaters, to the sound of spirited music, viewers could see Edison's *The Great Train Robbery,* the first great western classic. It begins with a view of a lonesome railroad telegraph station somewhere in the Rocky Mountains (actually, the film was shot at the Edison labs and in other locations in New Jersey). Two masked robbers enter the station and compel the train dispatcher to order the conductor of a train that has entered the station to take on water at this stop rather than the regular location farther down the line. The bandits tie and gag the station operator.

As the train leaves the water tank, the four bandits hop on board. Two overcome the express car messenger, blow up the strongbox with dynamite, take the mailbags and other valuables, and leave the car. The two others hold the engineer and fireman at gunpoint. When the fireman grabs a coal shovel to defend himself, he is thrown off the train. The bandits force the engineer to stop the train and uncouple the engine from the rest of the train.

The bandits force the passengers out of the coaches alongside the tracks and relieve them of their money and valuables. As one passenger foolishly makes an attempt to escape, he is shot down. Flush with cash, the bandits board the engine and force the engineer to help them make their escape down the tracks and farther into the mountains. Later, they leave the train for a prearranged hiding place.

The scene shifts back to the telegraph office, where the operator, still bound and gagged, manages to stumble to the table and reach his instruments. Despite the ropes he is able to wire for help before collapsing in exhaustion. Later, the operator's little daughter, delivering her father's lunch, finds him on the floor. She frees him and then runs for help at a nearby dance hall. The men inside the dance hall pick up their guns and head out after the robbers.

Soon, the bandits are seen dashing through the woods on spirited horses, closely followed by the sheriff and his posse. After much firing from both sides, one of the bandits is shot and falls from his horse. He gets back to his feet again and kills one of the posse before dying himself. A desperate battle now ensues between the surviving bandits and posse. Several men are killed.

The last scene shows a picture of the bandit chief filling the screen. He looks straight at the camera, takes his pistol, aims directly at the camera, and fires. That shot is so realistic, some observers later claim, that audiences always scream. Some even put their fingers in their ears to shut out the sound of the firing even though they are watching a silent movie.

A reporter from the *Philadelphia Inquirer* who saw the film in June 1904 wrote, "The Great Train Robbery has proven a thriller in nearly all the larger cities of the United States." The film, he said, was a source of wonder—those incredible scenes in the mountains, the action, the realism: "In the pursuit by the sheriff one is shot in the back as he dashes madly down hill, and the way in which he tumbles from his horse and strikes the ground leaves the spectators wondering if he is not a dummy, for it does not seem possible that a man could take such a fall and live."

From Tampa, Florida, a theater owner writes to the S. Lubin Life Motion Picture Machine Company in Philadelphia, a distributor, that the film is the greatest ever seen in Tampa. From St. Louis, another theater owner says the film is the biggest hit ever shown in Missouri. From Fort Worth, Texas; Birmingham, Alabama; Baltimore, Maryland; and St. James, Missouri, come similar plaudits. A man from Belleville, Ontario, has been showing two outlaw films, *The Great Train Robbery* and *The Bold Bank Robbery.* After showing the films at a fair, he writes, "The applause was something amazing. I really thought the grandstand had collapsed."

Numerous films about banditry and western crime appeared shortly after the turn of the century, films such as *Tracked by Bloodhounds, The Holdup of the Leadville Stage, Western Justice, Highway Robbery, The Great Mail Robbery, The Pay Train Robbery, The Robbery of the Citizens Bank,* and

The Bandit King. Although most of the films carried the moral message of law over lawlessness and the inevitable capture or killing of wrongdoers, the excitement and bravado of the outlaws filled theater seats. An advertising poster for a film in 1914 emblazoned these come-ons:

A DARING ROBBERY
A GREAT DETECTIVE STORY
A GANG OF CROOKS AND CUT THROATS
THE GREAT REVOLVER RIOT
THE MYSTERIOUS CRIMINAL

Psychologists, law enforcement and criminal experts, social scientists, and others began to express concern in learned journals and in popular magazines about this glorification of acts of outlawry, about the excitement and daring, which could be infectious to young minds. If Jesse, as the dime novelists had shown, was not entirely wrong in leading his life of danger, many other young Jesses out there in America might find a criminal life alluring. These films could be highly corruptive.

Mercury Pictures' *The Grey Fox,* the 1961 Canadian film portraying the life of Bill Miner, has the hero leaving San Quentin in 1901. Uncertain about his future, the aging bandit ends up in a theater. There, in the dark, with a piano furiously matching the intensity of the action, Bill watches the men on horseback battle the posse, watches the robbery and the chase, and feels the old emotions stirring. His eyes are intent; he begins to salivate. He knows what is in his own future. Old Bill was watching *The Great Train Robbery.*

With the advent of the motion picture industry, the leap from crook to legend became far easier. In 1908 the famous lawman Bill Tilghman made a movie about a bank robbery in Oklahoma. Bill found an extraordinarily appropriate leading man—former outlaw Al Jennings. Six years later, Tilghman made another film and found yet another former outlaw for the cast—Arkansas Tom, survivor of the Ingalls raid.

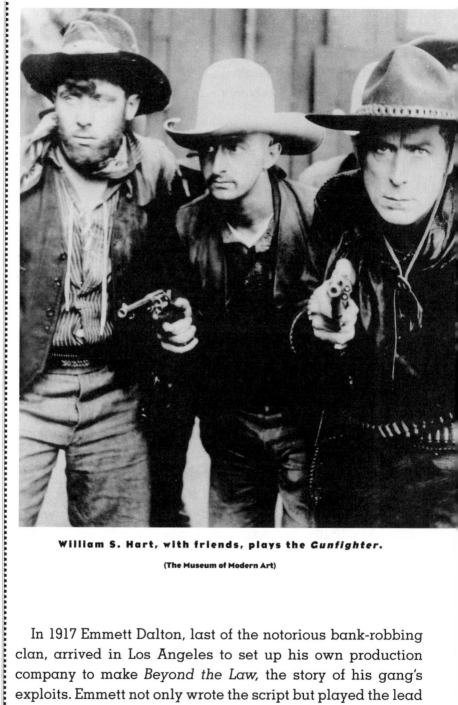

William S. Hart, with friends, plays the *Gunfighter*.

(The Museum of Modern Art)

In 1917 Emmett Dalton, last of the notorious bank-robbing clan, arrived in Los Angeles to set up his own production company to make *Beyond the Law,* the story of his gang's exploits. Emmett not only wrote the script but played the lead and strutted around the city with an ancient six-shooter swinging at his side.

In 1920, a company formed to produce a film about Jesse James. Several Kansas City businessmen, along with members of the James family, were stockholders. The filming was done in Missouri, on-site in Jackson, Clay, and Clinton counties. Playing Jesse James: Jesse Edwards James, son of the outlaw, a man once acquitted on a train-robbing charge in Kansas City. *Under the Black Flag* opened at a theater in Plattsburg, Missouri. Not surprisingly, the film emphasized the persecution that drove the young Jesse into banditry.

Seven years later, Paramount Pictures produced *Jesse James,* starring the famous actor Fred Thompson and his almost equally famous horse, Silver King. Jesse Edwards James was technical adviser this time around. The film, following the lead of most of the dime novels, caricatured Jesse as a modern-day Robin Hood. A writer for the *Kansas City Star,* aware that the James family was considering erecting a monument in Missouri to Jesse, said that the picture had made a good case for the monument. Fred Thompson said that after the first announcements of the picture had been made he was bombarded by letters from people who cherished Jesse's memory. Thompson seemed to know why. The James gang, he said, never robbed the poor and needy.

There would be other movies about Jesse. In 1939 Twentieth Century Fox and Darryl F. Zanuck released *Jesse*

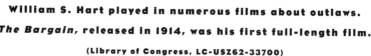

William S. Hart played in numerous films about outlaws. *The Bargain*, released in 1914, was his first full-length film.

(Library of Congress, LC-USZ62-33700)

James, with Tyrone Power playing Jesse and Henry Fonda as Frank. This was a film that portrayed the James brothers as courageous defenders of poor Missouri farmers against unscrupulous, predatory railroad interests who were buying up land at criminally low prices. Robert Wagner has also played Jesse. And in 1972, Philip Kaufman made *The Great Northfield, Minnesota, Raid,* starring Robert Duval and Cliff Robertson.

Many other movies about numerous bandit desperadoes would follow; they would make movie companies and actors rich. The genre of the misunderstood, complex loner, driven to violence by society's snares and outrages, the avenger of wronged peoples and institutions, would be replayed through the generations. From the days of the dime novel, the American outlaw hero has been a durable, resilient folk image.

"IMAGES OF THE WEST."

The painter Charles Schreyvogel on the roof of his apartment in Hoboken, New Jersey, 1903.

(National Cowboy Hall of Fame and Western Heritage Center)

Wild Bill Hickok, another Wild West hero featured in dime novels, was also a popular hero in movies and, later, television.

(National Archives, 111-SC-94122A)

Frank James in 1898, sixteen years after the death of Jesse and the end of the James gang.

(National Archives, 111-SC-93372)

This photograph, reproduced many times in articles and books about the West, was purportedly of Frank and Jesse James and Cole and Bob Younger. It was not. The picture is of four veterans of the Spanish-American War who posed for a photographer in Davenport, Iowa, shortly after the turn of the century. The boys enjoyed the hoax for years.

(Library of Congress, LC-USZ62-17001)

The real Cole Younger in Belton, Texas, 1906—in his sixties, a survivor long after his bandit days.

(Western History Collections, University of Oklahoma Library)

In 1918 Cole Younger smokes a pipe presented to him by the warden of the Stillwater Penitentiary, where he had spent much of his life after Northfield.

(Western History Collections, University of Oklahoma Library)

10

A NEW GENERATION

Alvin Karpis hides his face after his arrest in New Orleans, May 1936.

(National Archives, 65-H-130-3)

IN 1915 A BANK ROBBER NAMED HENRY STARR LED A GANG THAT ATTEMPTED TO ROB TWO BANKS IN STROUD, OKLAHOMA. THE ATTEMPTED DUAL FEAT WENT WELL ENOUGH UNTIL HENRY HEADED OUT OF TOWN. HE WAS FELLED BY A BULLET FROM A GUN wielded by a young boy. After spending several years in a prison in McAlester, Oklahoma, Starr attempted a robbery in Harrison, Arkansas, and was killed by a bank cashier. In 1915 Starr had ridden a horse into Stroud; in 1921 he drove an automobile into Harrison.

Al Spencer, cattle rustler and bank robber from Oklahoma, a member of Henry Starr's gang who had escaped after the Stroud robbery, read in a newspaper that he couldn't be considered in the same class with the Daltons or Bill Doolin, the revered names in Oklahoma banditry. After all, the newspaper writer pointed out, Spencer had never robbed a train. In 1923, along with several companions, he robbed a Missouri, Kansas & Texas Limited train near Okesa, Oklahoma. A few weeks later, he was killed near his hideout in the Osage Indian reservation by a posse led by a U.S. marshal.

A man named Roy Terrill, one of Al Spencer's lieutenants, took up his leader's mantle. Hooking up with Matt and George Kimes, Terrill accomplished an innovation in bank robbery. Instead of attempting to blow safes during robberies, Terrill, making use of twentieth-century technological progress, hauled the safes away in trucks to be opened later in relative safety. But Terrill's gang also succumbed to the lure of bandit immortality. Like the Daltons and Henry Starr, the Terrill gang members wanted to rob two banks at the same time. Like the Daltons, they failed and went out of business.

A new generation of American bandit gang leaders had been inspired by dime novels and movies and legendary stories. The times were different but the motivation was the same. Rise from obscurity and a life of routine; make a name; make money; flaunt obligation and rules and order; humble the advantaged; move with the fast and the tough and the loose; taste excitement and power.

For the new generation the targets were still mostly banks, the teams were still small gangs, and the tactics were still the hit-and-disappear guerrilla methods employed half a century earlier. But the new generation had the new tools. Eugene Gum, Secretary of the Oklahoma Bankers' Association, talked about the new gangs escaping in fast cars, filling the air with automatic weapons fire. In 1929, in California's Contra Costa County, bandits robbed a train using military-style machine gun emplacements.

Eugene Gum had a simple answer to this kind of violence: "Adopt a system of rewards for dead bandits and teach citizens how to shoot." A *New York Times* editorialist agreed: "The ever-ready automobile whisks them away to safety—it does, that is, unless instant action can be taken against them by their selected victim and his guards. If the latter can shoot, the hold-up trade becomes dangerous for its practitioners, for they know that whoever shoots at them will shoot to kill and will be praised in proportion to his skill."

The new generation of gangs featured numerous colorful characters. Arizona Donnie Clark Barker, better known as "Ma," a woman from the same region in Missouri that spawned Jesse and Frank James, gave birth to her gang—her four sons: Herman, Lloyd, Arthur (Doc) and Fred. The Barkers, too, were in the business of legend making. Not only did Ma and her four sons pull off numerous payroll, post office, and bank heists in the 1920s; she ran a refuge in Tulsa, Oklahoma, for escaped cons and other fugitives. The Barkers were high on the Justice Department's list of targets and the Feds later got most of them—Ma and Freddie, killed in a shootout at a lakeside cottage in Lake Weir, Florida; Doc, killed in an attempted escape from Alcatraz; Herman, killed by his own hand in 1927 after being severely wounded in a shootout in Kansas. Only Lloyd survived the law. He was killed later by his wife in a snack shop in California. Somehow Ma and her sons never learned death by natural causes.

George Kelly also became a legend. He could thank his wife, Kathryn, a gorgeous, black-haired woman from a poor farm family in Mississippi. Completely obsessed with visions of glamour, excitement, and power, Kate cavorted with a fast crowd of bootleggers and two-bit gamblers, finally hooking up with Kelly, a small-time booze runner in Memphis. Under Kate's tutelage, big George, practicing for hours under wilting Texas heat, became an expert marksman with the machine gun. Kelly once boasted that he could shoot walnuts off a fence at twenty-five yards and never damage the fence. When the two embarked on a bank-robbing and kidnapping career, they had the legend already marked out—"Machine Gun Kelly." After his arrest at a farm near Memphis, Tennessee, George spent most of the remaining years of his life in jail.

Clyde Barrow and Bonnie Parker—they didn't look like Warren Beatty and Faye Dunaway, who portrayed them decades later in *Bonnie and Clyde*; they also didn't have the savvy of John Dillinger, the true heir to Jesse's mantle of bank-robbing king. Dillinger called Bonnie and Clyde "a couple of punks" giving bank robbing a bad name. The two weren't simply misunderstood, mistreated victims of economic deprivation, Dillinger suggested; they were vicious, cruel killers who did it for kicks. But the nineteen-year-old Bonnie had a sense of history; she composed a poem called "The Story of Suicide Sal," an ode that, among other things, compared herself and her paramour favorably with Jesse James.

Frank Hamer, the former Texas Ranger who, with bloodhound determination, tracked the gang through Oklahoma and Missouri, ambushed them near Aracadia, Louisiana, in May 1934 and delivered them dead to the authorities. He declared, "I never had the slightest regret. I never killed anyone except human vermin that deserved killing. . . . I hated to have to shoot her, but, as they drove up that day and I pulled down on Barrow, knowing that some of my rifle bullets were going to snuff out her life along with his, I recalled how she had helped Barrow kill nine peace officers . . . you can't afford to feel mercy for such murdering rats, whether they are male or female." Congressman Thomas L. Blanton of Texas agreed: "Hamer's method is the quickest and most effective way of disposing of them. We do not capture alive and try rattlesnakes. We shoot their heads off before they strike." In the pair's bullet-riddled gray Ford coupe police found three Browning rifles, two Browning shotguns, eight automatic pistols, one revolver, and 2,000 rounds of ammunition.

Lester Gillis spent his entire life, it seemed, gaining revenge for all the beatings and snubbings he had endured as a young hood in a Chicago street gang. Short, almost sweet-looking, the kid found his equalizer in submachine guns and a hell-raising temper. For a time he worked for Al Capone in "labor relations" and toiled in the protection rackets of organized crime. As some of Lester's acquaintances recalled, he found psychopathic fulfillment in violence, in the sounds of gunfire, the sudden brushes with death, the victories, the power, all of it. Sent to Joliet after being captured in a small-time heist, he escaped and then launched his own independent career as a bandit leader. He hit several banks in Wisconsin, Iowa, and Nebraska. For a few months, until the final violence of his life, until being sprayed by seventeen bullets from the guns of federal agents near Barrington, Illinois, "Baby-Face Nelson" was Public Enemy Number One.

Alvin Karpis had also read the dime novels. The Canadian-born Karpis robbed, burgled, and kidnapped with the best, for a time running with the Barkers. Freddie Barker once called Karpis "Old Creepy" because of his constant dour expression; the sobriquet stuck. "My profession was robbing banks, knocking off payrolls, and kidnapping rich men. I was good at it," Creepy once said. But Alvin Karpis's criminal career ended with twenty-five years of hard time at Alcatraz. He was later deported.

In 1931, President Herbert Hoover, speaking at the convention of the International Police Chiefs Association, lamented the "sentimentalism in some people which makes popular heroes out of criminals." Hoover told the assembled lawmen that he looked forward confidently to the day when the moral forces in communities across America would rally to the side of the police against the criminal menace.

Shortly after Hoover's address, the historian James Truslow Adams, in a prophetic article published in the *New York Times* titled "Why We Glorify Our Gangsters," suggested that Hoover's dream was fanciful, that Americans would continue to like their heroes served up "picturesque and hot." Humanity, Adams wrote, craves heroes and legends. In the frontier setting of the post–Civil War West, there was an abundance of men whose lives depended on certain qualities usually inherent in folk heroes, qualities such as physical strength, recklessness, fearlessness, self-reliance, coolness under pressure, leadership, and personal magnetism. In the peculiar tumult of the West, it was sometimes difficult, Adams said, to draw the line between an honest frontiersman and a first-class criminal. The magnetic Jesse James, after all, was reckless, fearless, self-reliant, cool under pressure; and he was a leader.

Alvin Karpis wanted part of this hero action. So did John Dillinger and Charles Floyd.

"A New Breed"

Oklahoma bank robber Henry Starr, attempting with several companions to do what the Daltons could not do—successfully rob two banks at one time—also failed. In March 1915 he was shot off his horse by a seventeen-year resident of Stroud, Oklahoma, and went to jail for four years. After his release he made a movie of the ignominious effort called *Debtor to the Law*. Starr was later killed in Arkansas trying to rob another bank.

(National Archives, 111-SC-93346)

John Sontag and Chris Evans terrorized California's San Joaquin Valley in the early years of the twentieth century, robbing trains and stages. The end for Sontag came in the loose soil and brush of a farm field, where he had tried to shield himself from the gunfire of nearly two dozen members of a posse. When this picture was taken, Sontag was in the last minutes of his life.

(National Archives, 111-SC-93363)

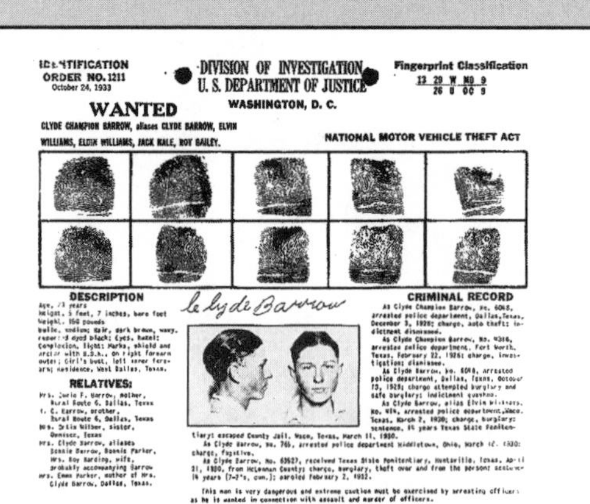

IDENTIFICATION ORDER NO. 1211
October 24, 1933

DIVISION OF INVESTIGATION
U. S. DEPARTMENT OF JUSTICE
WASHINGTON, D. C.

Fingerprint Classification
13 29 W MO 9
26 U OO 9

WANTED

CLYDE CHAMPION BARROW, aliases CLYDE BARROW, ELVIN WILLIAMS, ELDIN WILLIAMS, JACK HALE, ROY BAILEY.

NATIONAL MOTOR VEHICLE THEFT ACT

DESCRIPTION

Age, 23 years
Height, 5 feet, 7 inches, bare feet
Weight, 150 pounds
Build, medium; Hair, dark brown, wavy, reported dyed black; Eyes, hazel; Complexion, light; Marks, shield and anchor with U.S.N., on right forearm outer; Girl's bust, left inner forearm; Residence, West Dallas, Texas.

Clyde Barrow

RELATIVES:

Mrs. Cumie F. Barrow, mother, Rural Route 6, Dallas, Texas
L. C. Barrow, brother, Rural Route 6, Dallas, Texas
Mrs. Artie Wilber, sister, Denison, Texas
Mrs. Clyde Barrow, aliases Bonnie Barrow, Bonnie Parker, Mrs. Roy Harding, wife, probably accompanying Barrow
Mrs. Emma Parker, mother of Mrs. Clyde Barrow, Dallas, Texas.

CRIMINAL RECORD

As Clyde Champion Barrow, No. 6048, arrested police department, Dallas, Texas, December 3, 1926; charge, auto theft; indictment dismissed.

As Clyde Champion Barrow, No. 4316, arrested police department, Fort Worth, Texas, February 22, 1926; charge, investigation; dismissed.

As Clyde Barrow, No. 6048, arrested police department, Dallas, Texas, October 13, 1928; charge attempted burglary and safe burglary; indictment quashed.

As Clyde Barrow, alias Elvin Williams, No. 414, arrested police department, Waco, Texas, March 2, 1930; charge, burglary; sentence, 14 years Texas State Penitentiary; escaped County Jail, Waco, Texas, March 11, 1930.

As Clyde Barrow, No. 765, arrested police department Middletown, Ohio, March 12, 1930; charge, fugitive.

As Clyde Barrow, No. 63527, received Texas State Penitentiary, Huntsville, Texas, April 21, 1930, from McLennan County; charge, burglary, theft over and from the person; sentence 14 years (7-2's, con.); paroled February 2, 1932.

This man is very dangerous and extreme caution must be exercised by arresting officers as he is wanted in connection with assault and murder of officers.

Complaint was filed at Dallas, Texas, on May 20, 1933, charging Clyde Champion Barrow and Mrs. Roy Harding, nee Bonnie Parker, with transporting Ford Coupe, Motor No. A-1878100, property of Dr. E. L. Damron of Effingham, Illinois, from Dallas, Texas, to Pawhuska, Oklahoma, on or about September 16, 1932.

Law enforcement agencies kindly transmit any additional information or criminal record to nearest office, Division of Investigation, U. S. Department of Justice.

If apprehended, please notify the Director, Division of Investigation, U. S. Department of Justice, Washington, D. C., or the Special Agent in Charge of the office of the Division of Investigation listed on the back hereof, which is nearest your city.

(over) Issued by: J. EDGAR HOOVER, DIRECTOR.

Clyde Barrow wanted poster.

(National Archives, RG 60, DJ Classified Subject Files)

In 1930, Gus Winkler, bank robber and friend of Al Capone and other mob figures, relieved the Lincoln National Bank of more than $2 million. Arrested in Minnesota and extradited to Nebraska to stand trial, Gus leaves the Lincoln courthouse after posting bond on October 17, 1931.

(Nebraska State Historical Society)

In 1934, former Texas Ranger Frank Hamer came out of retirement at the request of the Texas governor to track down Bonnie and Clyde. He followed them to Louisiana and supervised their ambush on May 23.

(Western History Collections, University of Oklahoma Library)

11

CAPTURING BIG JOHN

Young John Dillinger at ten years of age in Indiana.

(National Archives, 306-NT-92650)

SOMEHOW IT ALL SEEMED INCONGRUOUS—JOHN DILLINGER AND HIS HENCHMEN (HARRY PIERPONT, CHARLEY MACKLEY, AND RUSSELL CLARK) AND HIS WOMEN FRIENDS (EVELYN FRECHETTE, MARY KINDER, AND OPAL LONG), HERE AMIDST THE saguaro cacti, the palm trees, the sweep of the Arizona desert, and the noble mountain backdrop. Dillinger in Tucson, "The Old Pueblo," away from the hustle of Chicago, away from the press of midwestern detectives and Justice Department snoops, away from the heat of the law to enjoy the heat of the winter southwestern sun.

* * * * * * *

Dillinger was the bandit king. After attending a movie in Washington in early 1934, a Justice Department official reported to his superiors about the reaction of the audience to a news clip on Dillinger. When the outlaw's picture first appeared on the screen, the audience roared its approval; when the images of Dillinger's parents then flashed on the screen, the audience cheered once again. So incensed did another department official become over this report that he angrily fired off a letter to the producer of the news clip, charging that the portrayal of Dillinger was biased in favor of the criminal, glorifying his horrendous deeds, making a

IDENTIFICATION ORDER NO. 1217
March 12, 1934.

DIVISION OF INVESTIGATION
U. S. DEPARTMENT OF JUSTICE
WASHINGTON, D. C.

Fingerprint Classification
12 9 R 0
14 U 00 9

WANTED

JOHN DILLINGER, with alias,
FRANK SULLIVAN

NATIONAL MOTOR VEHICLE THEFT ACT

DESCRIPTION

Age, 31 years
Height, 5 feet 7-1/8 inches
Weight, 153 pounds
Build, medium
Hair, medium chestnut
Eyes, grey
Complexion, medium
Occupation, machinist
Marks and scars, 1/2 inch scar back left hand; scar middle upper lip; brown mole between eyebrows
Mustache

Photograph taken January 25, 1934

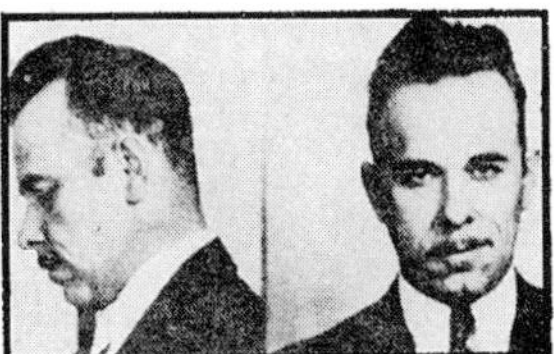

John Dillinger

CRIMINAL RECORD

As John Dillinger, #14395, received State Reformatory, Pendleton, Indiana, September 16, 1924; crime, assault and battery with intent to rob and conspiracy to commit a felony; sentences, 2 to 14 years and 10 to 20 years respectively;

As John Dillinger, #13225, received State Prison, Michigan City, Indiana, July 16, 1929; transferred from Indiana State Reformatory; paroled under Reformatory jurisdiction, May 10, 1933; parole revoked by Governor - considered as delinquent parolee;

As John Dillinger, #10587, arrested Police Department, Dayton, Ohio, September 22, 1933; charge, fugitive; turned over to Allen County, Ohio, authorities;

As John Dillinger, received County Jail, Lima, Ohio, September 28, 1933; charge, bank robbery; escaped October 12, 1933;

As Frank Sullivan, arrested Police Department, Tucson, Arizona, January 25, 1934; charge, fugitive; turned over to Lake County, Indiana, authorities;

As John Dillinger, #14487, arrested Sheriff's Office, Crown Point, Indiana, January 30, 1934; charge, murder - bank robbery; escaped March 3, 1934.

The United States Marshal, Chicago, Illinois, holds warrant of arrest charging John Dillinger with feloniously and knowingly transporting Ford V-8 four door sedan, motor number 256447, property of Lillian Holley, Sheriff, Lake County, Indiana, from Crown Point, Indiana to Chicago, Illinois, on or about March 3, 1934.

Law enforcement agencies kindly transmit any additional information or criminal record to the nearest office of the Division of Investigation, U. S. Department of Justice.

If apprehended, please notify the Director, Division of Investigation, U. S. Department of Justice, Washington, D. C., or the Special Agent in Charge of the Office of the Division of Investigation listed on the back hereof which is nearest your city

(over) Issued by: J. EDGAR HOOVER, DIRECTOR.

John Dillinger wanted poster.

(National Archives, RG 60, DJ Classified Subject Files)

heroic figure out of a crazed thug. Another Justice Department official couldn't believe the public response to Dillinger: "Applause, mind you, for a coward and a killer—applause for a man who had snuffed out the lives of husbands and fathers without the blinking of an eye—applause for one of the most loathsome creatures in the annals of crime." A writer for a national crime magazine, totally exasperated over the public's fascination with Dillinger, confessed that he could not understand the workings of the human mind. Another writer despaired at the "nauseating display of mushy sentimentality" infecting the public mind over such a cunning jackal.

With his taunting arrogance toward authority, his roadrunner dodges with the law, his audacious jail escapes, and his almost playful demeanor, Dillinger seemed to many in depression-ridden America as something of a romantic adventurer straight out of frontier legend, a poor boy beating the odds just as Jesse had done. To much of the public he seemed a threat only to the hated banks he robbed and the seemingly inept police he deceived.

As Dillinger toyed with his pursuers, the stakes for law enforcement officials to apprehend him increased each day. To allow the insolence of the arch-criminal to triumph would be to lose a measure of control over civic order. As an editorialist for the *Washington Post* remarked about Dillinger and his men: "The brazen insouciance and mocking ease with which the gang robbed and murdered, and then escaped, gave many a thoughtful person pause in contemplating a future of a country hapless in the face of such antisocial elements."

Born on June 22, 1903, son of an Indianapolis grocer, Dillinger dropped out of high school at age sixteen and worked for a time in a machine shop. When his father moved the family to a farm near Mooresville, Indiana, he began to get into trouble with the police. He joined the navy but soon jumped ship, returned home, married a sixteen-year-old girl, and began to hang around pool halls with small-time thieves. On September 6, 1924, he and a friend botched a robbery attempt of a grocer. Ten days later John ended up in the state reformatory in Pendleton, Indiana.

Later, Dillinger requested and was granted a transfer to the Indiana State Prison in Michigan City. He told prison authorities that he wanted to move to the prison to play on the baseball team. They believed him. The actual reason he wanted the transfer was to reunite with two felons he had befriended in Pendleton, men who had been sent earlier to

John Dillinger, 1934.

(National Archives, 306-NT-92649)

Michigan City—Harry Pierpont and Homer Van Meter.

Dillinger arrived in Michigan City on July 16, 1929, a young thief with an undistinguished crime record, one of thousands of inmates in Michigan City over the years, one, as all the others, photographed with the front view and the profile and the number underneath, just another jammed into the crowded mess halls. Little did the guards or the wardens or the fellow inmates know of the fame that was in his future.

In Michigan City, Pierpont and Van Meter introduced Dillinger to John Hamilton and other veteran bank robbers. They gave him lessons; he gave them visions. Dillinger emerged from prison in 1933 as if reborn, turning himself from a two-bit unknown into a daring, machine-gun-toting gangster. He had learned from Hamilton and the others but soon became their leader. He left prison on a mission to make of himself something big.

The nucleus of the gang included the seasoned and tough ex-cons—Hamilton, Van Meter, Tommy Carroll, and Eddie Green—men who could get guns and doctors and women, could case banks and fight like madmen. The gang stormed across the Midwest pulling off stunning daylight attacks and then, almost magically, disappearing. Wearing a white straw boater and a jaunty, wide grin, Dillinger often traded quips with bank employees and customers and always entertained them all with his trademark, an athletic leap over the teller's counter.

As Jesse had learned from Quantrill and Bloody Bill Anderson, the guerrilla must strike lightning fast and disappear, hit at all hours, and not be predictable. Dillinger baffled those on his trail, hiding in places like St. Paul, a place where, for a price, police kept looking the other way. He disappeared in Chicago's seedy netherworld of bars and dives and hangouts. He dodged and escaped and stole more money in twelve months than Jesse had stolen in sixteen years.

Many women were captivated. He loved some, cavorted with many. Evelyn Frechette was his favorite. A gorgeous, black-haired member of the Menonomie Indian tribe in Wisconsin, Evelyn had been a waitress and saleswoman and was married to an inmate at Alcatraz named Welton Sparks. When she met Dillinger in a Chicago café in the fall of 1933, she didn't know his background and reputation; when she found out, it made the love affair even more exhilarating. A Justice Department report on the Dillinger gang described Evelyn as being of the "hard boiled, gangster, moll type of woman, who consorted with, aided, abetted, and in general harbored and concealed members of one of the most desperate gangs in the United States . . . she is of the thrill-seeking type. Her attitude and demeanor reflect viciousness." To John Dillinger she was an exciting, loyal comrade.

A group of women constantly accompanied the gang in their peripatetic movements around the country. In addition to Evelyn there were Mary Kinder, Opal Long, Mary Longnaker, Dorothy Sherrington, and several others who often acted as advance agents for the gang, renting houses and apartments, buying automobiles, even finding weapons. As liaisons and messengers, they were useful allies; as lovers and accomplices they fired the spirit of the outlaw king, made him seem more carefree. But one of them would trade for his life.

Dillinger collected weapons and assorted battle accoutrements the way some people collected coins or stamps. He had .38-caliber superautomatic pistols, Thompson submachine guns, leather shoulder holsters, bulletproof vests, and assorted other handguns and rifles. But Dillinger was much more than a two-bit thug with war-making capability; he was suave, even sophisticated, a con man. He sometimes cased banks disguised as a nun. He once passed himself off as a banker interested in preventing robberies and was so successful at gaining the cooperation of several midwestern bankers that they feted him at a luncheon. Dillinger later visited each of the banks, shared information about how to thwart crime, and then, using the information he had gained on each of the individual banks to good advantage, robbed them.

Dillinger once posed as a reporter for a crime magazine. Walking into a police precinct, he gained the confidence of several policemen, began asking questions about how they intended to catch Dillinger, and listened as they revealed to him the weapons and plans they had in mind. A few days later, Dillinger and his men raided the precinct and stole much of its arsenal.

Through the fall of 1933 and winter of 1934, the nation's chief bandit machine-gunned and finessed his way out of ambushes and traps and police plottings. The gang lost some men, but took out some policemen in several violent exchanges. Through all of the attention the man from Indiana was having a marvelous time. He had the eye of the public, the press, the government; and he was now in the gorgeous Southwest to spend some time recouping energies and enjoying some of his earnings with his men and his molls.

On January 22, 1934, they checked into the old Congress Hotel, a Tucson landmark, its Spanish flavor a welcome change from the flops of the big cities and the tacky sameness of the small-town dives where the gang had often sought refuge. They had driven into Tucson in a brand-new 1934 Studebaker Club Sedan, a 1934 Buick, and a 1934 Hudson Club Sedan. Into the hotel the gang carried fine-quality suitcases filled with clothes, maps, handguns, submachine guns, bulletproof vests, and money, much money. Accompanying the group was a Boston terrier. In Tucson the temperature was in the balmy sixties, compared to frigid Chicago, where paralyzing winds whipped in from the lake. The Dillinger gang had earned a vacation.

But shortly after the gang checked in, a fire broke out in the Congress Hotel. Charley Mackley and Russell Clark, in their rooms when the fire began, gathered together the luggage, bulging with their arsenal and loot, hauled it to a fire ladder that had been quickly erected to the Tenth Street side of the hotel, and handed the pieces to firemen Bill Benedict, Kenneth Pender, and Bob Freeman. Although slightly blackened from the smoke, the suitcases, along with their owners, made it to safety. One of the outlaws handed the firemen some money as a token for the rescue. One fireman noted the particular anxiety of the two guests and the exceptional weight of the suitcases.

The following day, the firemen, lounging around the fire station reading detective magazines, were startled. Of interest was an article on the fearsome Dillinger gang, replete with pictures of the various members. Those two guys yesterday at the hotel, the guys with the heavy suitcases and the tips . . . those faces in the magazine . . .

Into the Tucson police department marched the firemen with one of the hottest stories ever to hit town. After the firemen correctly identified mug shots from the department's files, the police eagerly took up the trail. John Dillinger and his crew once again were the targets of a manhunt, this time in the desert Southwest. But in this region of gila monsters and scorpions, police instincts were not appreciably different from those of cops in Manhattan or Chicago, even if the Tucson police department was not even equipped with a police radio system.

They began to investigate recent rentals of properties in the city against deliveries of baggage from the Congress Hotel. At 927 North Second Avenue, a few blocks from the University of Arizona, a couple of miles from downtown Tucson, a group of men and women had rented a small house and were driving new cars with out-of-state license plates. After a brief stakeout, the police matched faces with mug shots.

Early on Thursday, January 25, four officers approached the single-story home on Second Avenue. Carrying a newspaper in his hand, feigning he was lost and trying to find an address, Chet Sherman reached the door, only to discover that the ruse had not worked. Seeing Russell Clark bolt to the door, Sherman drew his pistol. Clark opened the door and grabbed Sherman's arm. The two struggled across the room into the adjacent bedroom, the plucky officer holding on for dear life against his much stronger opponent. Clark lost by

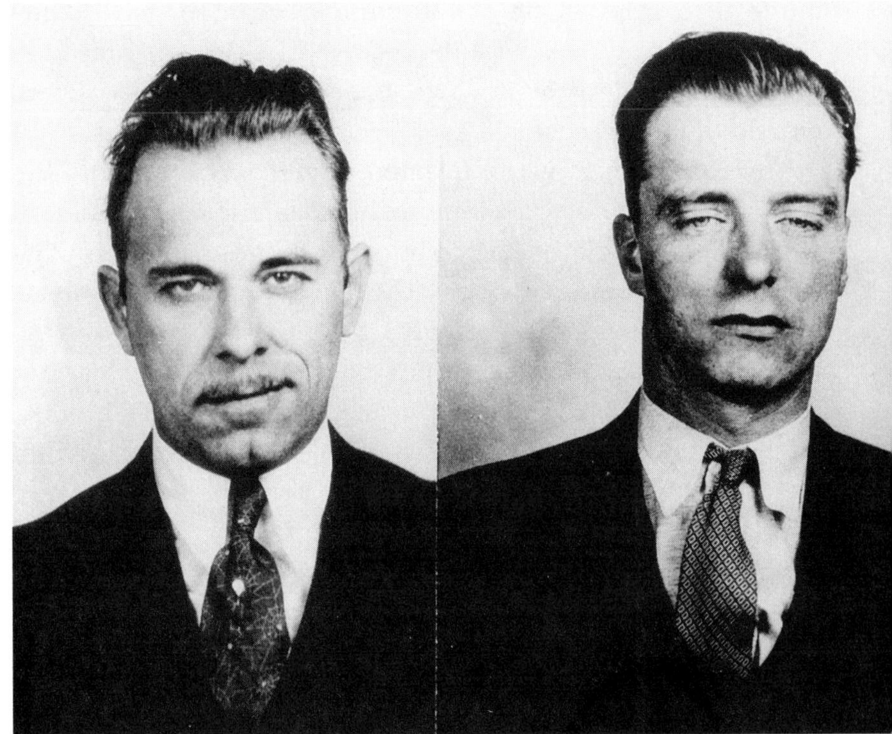

Mug shots taken by Tucson, Arizona, police of John Dillinger, Harry Pierpont, and Charles Mackley, January 1934.

(Arizona Historical Society/Tucson, B Port Dillinger 28,161)

force of numbers as a pistol from one of the other officers came crashing down on his head.

Shortly after Clark had been subdued, Charley Mackley was picked up while browsing in the nearby Grabe Electric Company. While officers were booking and fingerprinting their two captives, motorcycle patrolman Earl Nolan had followed a car bearing a Florida license plate into an auto court at South Sixth Avenue and Nineteenth Street. Alerting other officers, Nolan approached a tall, slender, scholarly-looking man wearing glasses. Nolan and the others persuaded the gentleman to accompany them to headquarters. As they entered the station, the man suddenly whirled and pulled a gun from his belt. He quickly dropped it when a shotgun from

one of the officers pressed against his skull. Harry Pierpont, called "Killer" by some in the profession, the triggerman of the Dillinger gang, was now in custody. He wasn't happy. Coolly looking over the Tucson cops, Pierpont sneered. "I'll remember you—and you—and you," he said. "I can get out of any jail. I'll be back and I'll not forget."

Back at the Second Street house, officers waited in the dark. When the Hudson pulled up and its driver, along with a woman companion, approached the house, the police surrounded them. Although the man's first instinct was to go for the pistol in his coat, he quickly realized the folly of such a move and affably gave up. Sprightly stepping into police headquarters, Dillinger talked breezily and freely. He almost seemed amused, caught here in Tucson by these small-town officers. Around the room he saw scattered the gang's suitcases, trunks, machine guns, piles of steel-jacketed bullets, steel vests, and one Boston terrier puppy. The police also found over $25,000 in cash.

From Indiana, Ohio, Wisconsin, and Illinois, the Tucson police received telegrams and calls from law enforcement officials who wanted the fugitives. Ohio eventually won the right to try Clark and Mackley for murder; Indiana won the rights to Dillinger. The Justice Department's Division of Investigation also arrived in Tucson to question the captives about a kidnapping case. This was one crime, however, for which John Dillinger could forthrightly claim total innocence.

The city of Tucson was agog. On January 26, 1934, at 9:30 A.M., an estimated crowd of two thousand milled outside the downtown justice court building while inside a battery of

Dillinger gang captives hide faces at arraignment in Tucson.

(Arizona Historical Society/Tucson, B Port Dillinger 28,163)

cameras flashed at the four handcuffed male prisoners and the three women who were not manacled. At the arraignment, the gang members were held under $100,000 bonds as fugitives from justice for a series of robberies and murders. Those Tucson citizens lucky enough to have gotten a courtroom seat recognized Dillinger immediately from all of the photos, news clips, and wanted posters saturating the country. Newspapers that day filled column after column with photographs of the prisoners, minute descriptions of the apprehensions, lists of the outlaws' alleged depredations, even a page in one paper entitled "Bits of This And That In Capture of Dillinger Gang," a potpourri of items, including a complete description of the gang's luggage and the jewelry of the women.

Local editorialists gleefully hailed their city's conquering heroes: "The hick town police didn't know anything about policing. You see, they had not learned under the Al Capone influence in Chicago and other Midwest centers. They had an idea that a gangster was a bad citizen and should be arrested. They must have been reading dime detective novels or something, or they would never have gone back to the hideout and waited. If John Dillinger had thought they would, he wouldn't. But he did. And now he is with his companions in the county jail."

After the passions of the arrest gave way to reflection, Harry Pierpont also sang the praises of the Tucson police. These were not hick cops, the triggerman said, but "the smartest officers I've ever seen." Realizing that he could have easily been killed in the police station when he pulled his gun, Pierpont said that the officer who had jammed the shotgun at his head "was a swell fellow not to shoot me . . . if all this had happened in Ohio, we'd be lying on a slab."

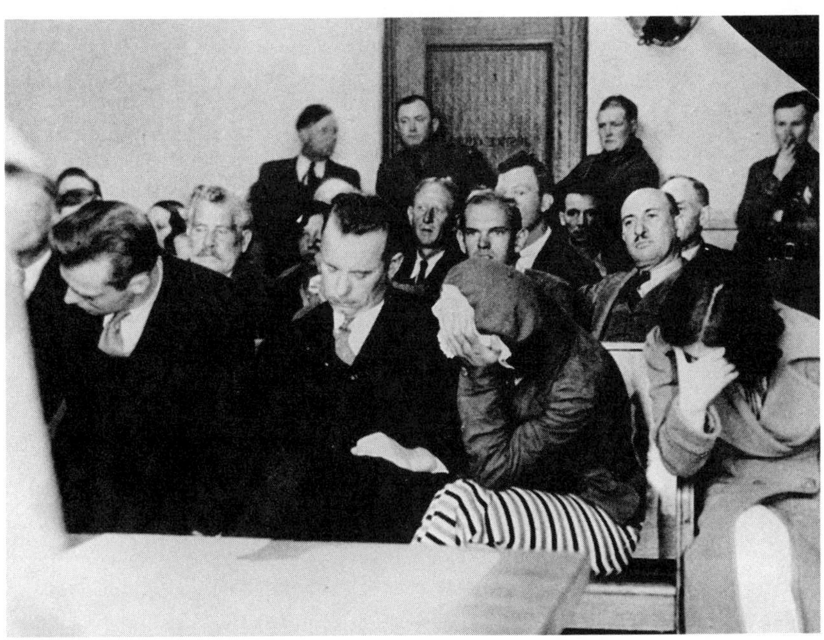

Members of John Dillinger's gang at arraignment in Tucson, Arizona, 1934—left to right: Harry Pierpont, Dillinger, Ann Martin, and Mary Kinder.

(National Archives, 306-NT-92651)

Tucson police officers pose with weapons taken from the Dillinger gang.

(Arizona Historical Society/Tucson, B Port Dillinger)

At the jail, the officers and the infamous crooks got along famously. One of the policemen brought the Boston terrier and the men struck up a conversation. Charley Mackley tried to explain his life: "Look at my dad. He worked like the devil all his life and what did he get out of it? I have lived as long in forty minutes at times as my dad did in forty years. It's all what you make it, and sometimes it's a close decision."

It seemed as if all of Tucson wanted to see Dillinger, and the police chief accommodated them; he put the crooks on display. At the Pima County Courthouse on Sunday and Monday, Sheriff John Belton escorted men, women, and children in groups up into the jail area and paraded them past the cells.

At the Southern Pacific station on January 30, over a thousand people watched as Dillinger and his henchmen were finally turned over to Indiana authorities. They were hustled back to the Midwest for trial. Two of the three women were released in Tucson. Back at the house on North Second Avenue, college kids and other curiosity seekers slowly drove by pointing . . . "Is this the place?"

At the Crown Point jail in Indiana, which many officers claimed was escape proof, Dillinger jocularly posed for a photograph arm in arm with warden Lillian Holley and prosecuting attorney Robert Estill. The photo appeared in newspapers across the country, much to the discomfort of Indiana authorities. The photo became even more embarrassing a short time later. On March 3, 1934, Dillinger escaped again. This time he used a fake wooden gun carved from a washboard, disarmed prison guards, and drove away in the warden's car. As he crossed the Illinois state line he violated the Dyer Act against interstate auto theft, thus bringing the Justice Department's Bureau of Investigation into the Dillinger manhunt.

A few days later, Dillinger posed in front of his friends for another picture, holding the wooden gun in one hand and clutching a machine gun with the other. From such photos does mythology grow, and Dillinger was acutely aware of the possibilities. He wrote a note to his sister: "I thought I would write a few lines and let you know I am still percolating. Don't worry about me, honey, for that don't help any, and besides I am having a lot of fun. . . . I locked eight deputies and a dozen trusties up with my wooden gun before I got my hands on two machineguns and you should have seen their faces. Ha! Ha! Ha! . . . "

"THE HUNT FOR PUBLIC ENEMY NUMBER ONE"

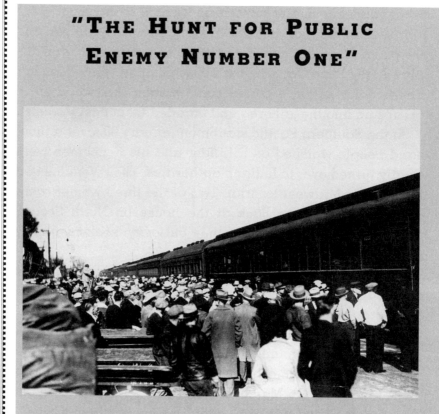

TOP: John Dillinger was an enormous public attraction. Crowds gather at a Tucson train station as police prepare to take the prisoner to Indiana.

(Arizona Historical Society/Tucson, B Port Dillinger 28, 164)

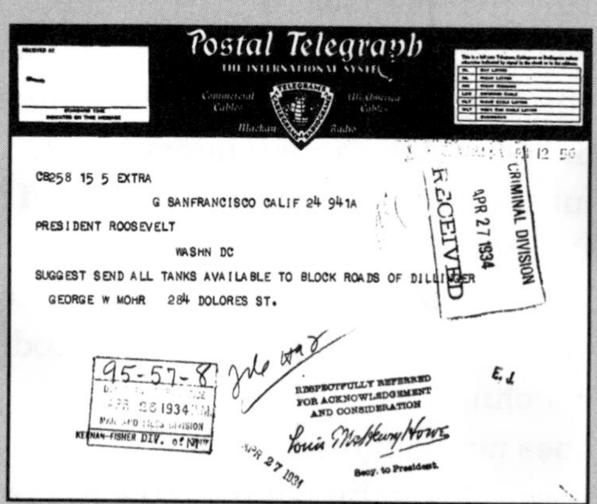

Postal Telegraph
THE INTERNATIONAL SYSTEM
Commercial Cables — All America Cables — Mackay Radio

CB258 15 5 EXTRA

G SANFRANCISCO CALIF 24 941A

PRESIDENT ROOSEVELT

WASHN DC

SUGGEST SEND ALL TANKS AVAILABLE TO BLOCK ROADS OF DILLINGER

GEORGE W MOHR 284 DOLORES ST.

RECEIVED APR 27 1934 CRIMINAL DIVISION

95-57-8

APR 26 1934 P.M.

KEENAN-FISHER DIV. of NPT

RESPECTFULLY REFERRED FOR ACKNOWLEDGEMENT AND CONSIDERATION

Louis McHenry Howe

Secy. to President.

APR 27 1934

ABOVE: The Roosevelt administration in Washington got advice and warnings from all over the United States on ways to deal with John Dillinger. This gentleman wanted the intervention of the army.

(National Archives, RG 60, DJ Classified Subject Files)

RIGHT: One of the FBI's official portraits of J. Edgar Hoover. (National Archives, 306-PSA-59-21536)
BOTTOM: Hotel at Spider Lake, Wisconsin, from which Dillinger, warned by a barking dog, made a spectacular escape from police and federal agents. (National Archives, 306-NT-92488)

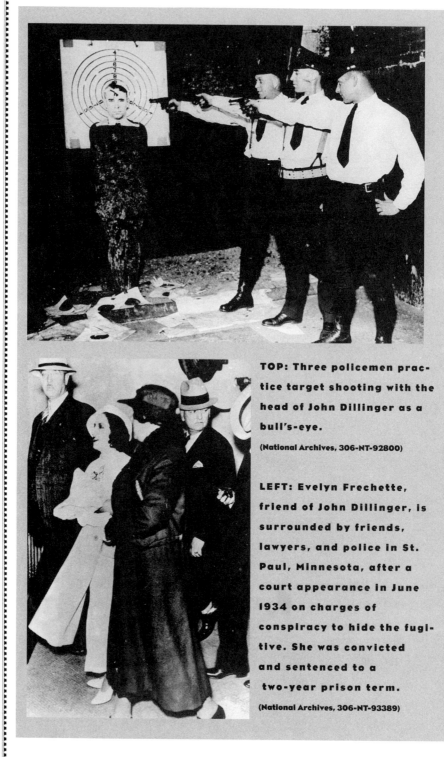

TOP: Three policemen practice target shooting with the head of John Dillinger as a bull's-eye.

(National Archives, 306-NT-92800)

LEFT: Evelyn Frechette, friend of John Dillinger, is surrounded by friends, lawyers, and police in St. Paul, Minnesota, after a court appearance in June 1934 on charges of conspiracy to hide the fugitive. She was convicted and sentenced to a two-year prison term.

(National Archives, 306-NT-93389)

John Dillinger shows off a machine gun and the wooden pistol he claimed he used to hoodwink Indiana prison guards.

(Indiana Division, Indiana State Library)

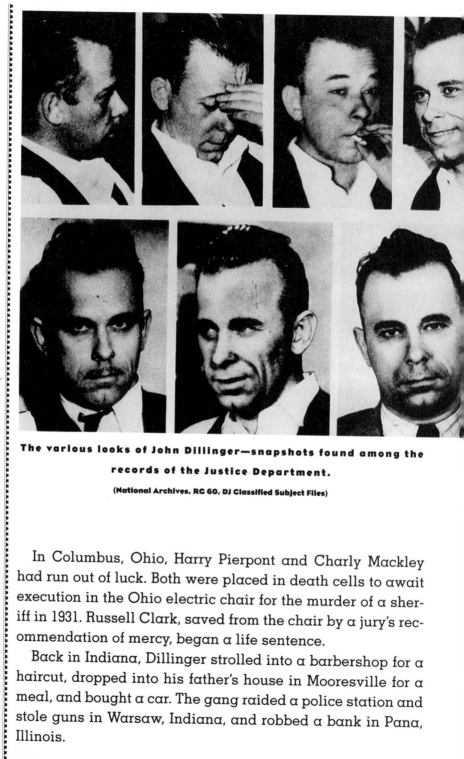

The various looks of John Dillinger—snapshots found among the records of the Justice Department.

(National Archives, RG 60, DJ Classified Subject Files)

In Columbus, Ohio, Harry Pierpont and Charly Mackley had run out of luck. Both were placed in death cells to await execution in the Ohio electric chair for the murder of a sheriff in 1931. Russell Clark, saved from the chair by a jury's recommendation of mercy, began a life sentence.

Back in Indiana, Dillinger strolled into a barbershop for a haircut, dropped into his father's house in Mooresville for a meal, and bought a car. The gang raided a police station and stole guns in Warsaw, Indiana, and robbed a bank in Pana, Illinois.

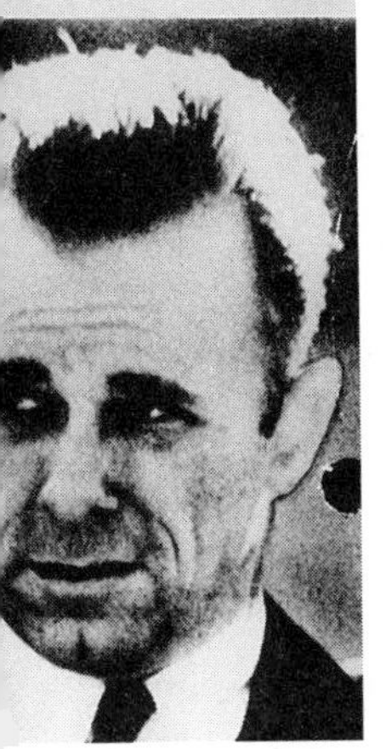

Congressmen and senators railed against Dillinger's reign of crime. Editorialists found him a lively topic; civic officials found him a source of worry and chagrin. Humorists discovered in his exploits a rich source of quips. Will Rogers suggested that the police were perhaps using too many men to track him down. Two hundred armored cars can't sneak up on nobody, Will said. In the old days it was one Pinkerton detective or one Ranger who dropped the evil badman: "I bet we got a lot of good man hunters in our various forces, if they were allowed to work without carrying an orchestra with 'em."

From coast to coast, people reported seeing Dillinger. Eyewitnesses to a robbery in South Dakota decided that the crooks were probably Dillinger and his boys. The next day citizens in the Bronx claimed to have seen Dillinger in a car with Illinois plates. Another day later, folks in upper New York State saw the gang leader, and so did some people in Chicago—at a gas station, at a Cubs game, and in a bar. Also in Chicago, a paper reported that Dillinger had been seen shooting a dog in a local park. Dillinger, at the time in a Daytona Beach, Florida, hotel reading an article on the supposed sighting in Chicago, said to his girlfriend, "That couldn't have been me; I can't shoot that far."

Even in Britain, Dillinger was major news. Impressed by Dillinger's ability to elude captors, a British newspaper suggested that Indians were aiding the famous fugitive. Some Scotland Yard detectives swore that Dillinger had been seen walking the streets of London. And an English innkeeper phoned the bobbies to report that several of the Dillinger gang, at that very moment, were in his establishment drinking beer; they turned out to be Rhodes scholars from the United States. A correspondent to a London paper said that Americans were suffering a bad attack of "the Dillinger jitters."

In the U.S. House of Representatives, a congressman from West Virginia, Jennings Randolph, declared, "Throughout America millions of alarmed citizens are waiting and watching for the outcome of the Dillinger escapades. . . . When wild animals become too abundant and destructive to property, the State declares open season on them, which means that they are shot at sight by persons who enjoy the kill." Dillinger's head and pelt, suggested Mr. Randolph, were now on the line.

Writing from a hotel on West Madison Street in Chicago, a "Physiogonomist and Trance Medium" named Prince De Vonis, a man who claimed he could drive a car on a busy street blindfolded, also offered his services. The prince, who had demonstrated his telepathic powers in theaters from Iowa to Montana and had aided local police in other crime operations, said he could get the Dillinger outfit "tied up in a short time."

Time magazine turned the Dillinger hunt into a colorful board game called "Dillinger Land." The game featured a dotted line marking the reported trails of the fugitive as well as skulls indicating the sites where lawmen or Dillinger henchmen had died.

Crime magazines and tabloids filled column after column with the Dillinger gang's escapades. Various state and local police agencies set up special Dillinger units to deal with the menace. He was one of the nation's most notable figures. The *Literary Digest* called Dillinger "the country's worst outlaw since Jesse James."

In Washington, at their new building on Pennsylvania Avenue, Justice Department officials approached the Dillinger case as the greatest challenge facing American law enforcement. Attorney General Homer Cummings declared that America was strangling in a swarm of gangsters, racketeers, dope dealers, kidnappers, swindlers, bootleggers, and roving gangs of bank robbers led by such characters as Pretty Boy Floyd, Baby-Face Nelson, and, worst of all, Dillinger. Killing a man in America, said the irascible

Baltimore journalist Henry L. Mencken, was safer "than in any other civilized society."

From a survey of 130 cities in the United States in 1932, the combined homicide rate totaled one person to each ten thousand. For the same period in England, Scotland, and Wales, the rate was one for each two hundred thousand. In the five years from 1929 to 1934, there were nearly 3,500 bank robberies in the United States, or nearly two a day. The cashier of a small bank in Kansas wrote to President Roosevelt that machine gun bank banditry attacks in his state had nearly ruined the banking industry. "It is," he said, "getting to be a matter of Life and Death."

From across the country came plans and suggestions to the attorney general on how to deal with men such as Dillinger. One individual demonstrated in a diagram how a trapdoor should be placed in front of every cashier's window in every bank in the country. When a holdup man such as Dillinger appeared in front of the window, the teller would push a button releasing the trap, thereby propelling the robber downward into a large net that would close around the prey.

One writer suggested that all criminals should be tattooed with different marks indicating their crime specialties. Another writer suggested that all running boards and handles on cars be retractable so that crooks could not hold on to the sides of moving cars.

"Skunk Oil Vapor Spray"—that was the answer, suggested still another. Every payroll desk and bank window should have nearby a high-pressure can of the stuff to shoot at the bags of money and at thieves like Dillinger. "Besides," said the writer, "it will make a new Industry raising the skunks for this purpose."

Faced with growing demands from the public that the Justice Department find a way to bring down Dillinger, also faced with the spectacle of Dillinger's becoming something of a folk hero, the attorney general and the head of the Justice Department's investigative division, J. Edgar Hoover, embarked on a crusade not only to kill Dillinger but to change public attitudes about criminals. He launched a public relations drive to replace the "cult of the criminal" with the "cult of the G-Man." Dillinger was not Robin Hood, government officials asserted; he was a marauding, petty hood.

Assistant Attorney General James Keenan declared in a speech at a governors' conference: "From the days of the Wild West and the escapades of the notorious James brothers . . . the public in general has seemed to engender an interest—much the same as they enjoy reading a detective story." The grim side, the reality of crime and death, he said, seemed somehow lost in myth and romanticism.

The setback in Tucson had only fueled Dillinger's determination to make a national mockery of law enforcement. The *Baltimore Sun* accommodated him: "If nothing else, the depredations and journeys of Mr. Dillinger make the police look a trifle silly." The *Cleveland Plain Dealer* concurred: Dillinger had superior intelligence, said the editorialist, but his reputation "is based mainly upon the fact that the law has been extraordinarily dumb." A writer for a national magazine called Dillinger's braggadocio and buffoonery "a national humiliation."

Attorney General Homer Cummings vowed a massive government assault against Dillinger and the other hoods. The running board bank robbers who had thrived in a twilight zone of inaction and confusion would be an endangered species, he promised. Cummings proposed a whole battery of new laws to expand federal jurisdiction and to increase the power of federal prosecutors. He talked of a national police force, acting in concert with state and local forces, to crush society's lawless elements, a mighty investigative team armed with a sophisticated array of radio, telegraph, telephone, photograph, and fingerprint capability, marshaling the latest scientific advances in criminal detection. Some magazine and newspaper writers began to refer to Cummings's vision as the "American Scotland Yard."

On May 19, 1934, four months after John Dillinger had been

captured in Tucson, two months after his wooden gun escape in Crown Point, Indiana, President Franklin Roosevelt signed six crime bills expanding federal authority. The president declared, "Law enforcement and gangster extermination cannot be made completely effective so long as a substantial part of the public looks with tolerance upon known criminals . . . or applauds efforts to romanticize crime." In a hyperbolic flourish, Cummings claimed in a speech that the crime underworld had more men with arms than the combined forces of the United States Army and Navy. The government, he said, needed reinforcements and was now getting them. And the first and most important order of business to demonstrate federal power was to bring down the crafty Indiana hoodlum who was making a mockery of law enforcement. If local law enforcement officials in Tucson, Arizona, could capture Johnny D., certainly the Justice Department could silence him forever.

Dillinger now faced a formidable adversary in the director of the Justice Department's Division of Investigation, a man who would be as legendary in his own profession as Dillinger had become in his. At an old-fashioned frame house at 423 Seward Square in Washington, J. Edgar Hoover lived quietly with his aging mother. Down on Pennsylvania Avenue, in a palatial, oak-paneled suite, he was the nation's prime crook catcher.

His first job had been as a clerk at the Library of Congress cataloging new books. At night, he attended law school at George Washington University, eventually earning a degree. In 1917 he took a job at the Department of Justice as a clerk, and within two years had been made a special assistant to Attorney General A. Mitchell Palmer. Soon, Hoover was handed a big case, a case full of lusty newspaper copy, of heated national debate, and of wartime emotion. The young assistant took over the prosecution of the deportation proceedings against the anarchist Emma Goldman. Here was the young Hoover against one of the country's most loved and despised radicals, a left-wing spear-carrier. Hoover leaped into the job with crusading zeal. In a drizzling early morning rain in December 1919, Emma and other anarchists sailed from Ellis Island in New York headed to Russia; Hoover stood on the dock smiling.

The Goldman case rocketed Hoover into national prominence and into the highest echelon of government civil service. And now, John Dillinger had come into his life. Just as Emma Goldman had, Dillinger gave Hoover a chance for glory, an opportunity to propel his career forward. "Stay on Dillinger," Hoover ordered his agents. "Go anywhere the trail takes you."

Out in Austin, Texas, a former Texas Ranger named Frank Hamer, who had brought an end to the sordid saga of Bonnie Parker and Clyde Barrow, now announced that he was ready to bring an end to Dillinger. "I can deliver Dillinger in the same way I did Clyde and Bonnie," he said. "Dead. You wouldn't think I'd expect to take Dillinger alive, would you?"

Hoover and his agents ignored the Texas lawman; they wanted the honors. Through the spring of 1934, the agents tried to do what local authorities in Tucson had done—find "Public Enemy Number One." They sifted through tips, set traps, and looked for the right opportunity to strike. Unlike the Tucson police, however, the Feds did not aim simply to arrest the arch-criminal but, just as Hamer had suggested, to exterminate him. In Baltimore, the acerbic journalist Henry L. Mencken agreed: "No effort could reform such men as Dillinger and any effort to do so is a sheer waste of time and money." Dillinger and his ilk were incurably criminal, said Mencken, "and the only rational way to deal with them is to put them to death."

When federal agents and National Guard and state police surrounded a northern Wisconsin resort called Little Bohemia, the press in Washington was summoned to the Justice Department. The fox was trapped, Hoover said. Accompanied by his aides and eager newspapermen, the Director awaited word from the Wisconsin woods. But the news that night would not please Hoover. Warned by barking watchdogs, Dillinger escaped from Little Bohemia. In the confusion of the battle one of three workers from a nearby CCC camp who was fleeing the scene died in a hail of police bullets. A federal agent lost his life a few hours later while chasing the gang. The killer was identified as Lester Gillis, better known as "Baby-Face Nelson." Nelson had recently joined the Dillinger gang.

In Chicago, at the Bankers Building, agent Melvin Purvis directed local operations. A veteran investigator from South Carolina, short and frail-looking, almost always sporting an exceptionally large, flat straw hat that obscured everything down to eye level, Purvis was a dogged stalker. He and Hoover soon decided to focus on Chicago, which Dillinger often used as a base. With its elaborate train system, its maze of towering buildings and swarming streets, and the road arteries toward adjacent states, Chicago had offered Dillinger a haven for years. But Purvis was confident he could flush him out. "Man-hunting isn't a game," he said. "It's a grim and tragic affair . . . man-hunting is war, without quarter or kindness and . . . the finer points of the code duello aren't likely to worry you much."

On July 21, the Justice Department team, working with local Chicago and Indiana police, got a big break, a tip from one Anna Sage, owner of an East Chicago brothel. Anna was facing federal deportation charges and wanted reward money and a promise of help from the Immigration Bureau for her information. She told Purvis that she and a friend would accompany Dillinger the next night to a movie; Purvis told his men that another Dillinger escape would make the new war on crime look ludicrous.

While Hoover paced the floor of his library at 413 Seward Square in Washington, receiving minute-by-minute updates from the stakeout, Dillinger and two women watched a film called *Manhattan Melodrama,* starring Clark Gable. After the movie ended, as Dillinger and the two women walked outside into the sweltering summer night, Melvin Purvis, signaling his team of agents in the dark, lit up a cigar.

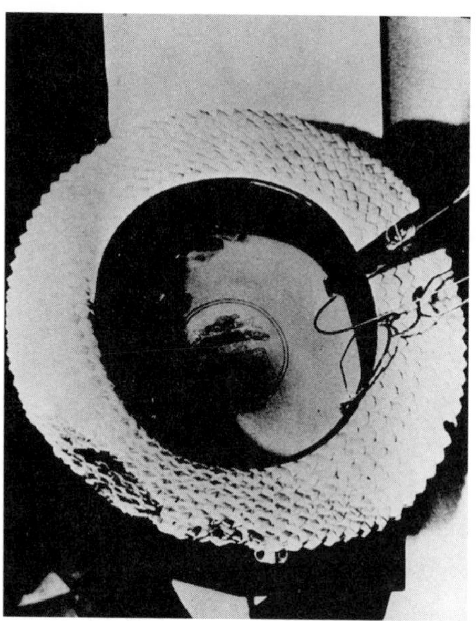

The personal effects of Dillinger, photographed after his death in Chicago—hat, eyeglasses, and cigar.

(National Archives, 306-NT-94982)

The manhunt ended as Hoover had hoped. At an alley entrance near Chicago's Biograph Theater, in a bullet firestorm, Dillinger died. It was not a shootout; Dillinger did not have time to draw his gun. As his body lay on the sidewalk spilling blood, onlookers dipped their handkerchiefs into the pools for souvenirs. Dillinger was no longer Public Enemy Number One; he was morgue case "July-116."

The *Chicago Daily News* gave the fall of Dillinger and his gang its greatest animal imagery prose: "They wanted to be heroes. They were hoodlums. They wanted to be admired. They were despised. They wanted to be thought brave, but what is bravery? The lion is brave; the bull elk is brave; the hyena and the jackal are merely desperate."

The Feds had their kill. They now prepared for the next step in the war on crime, a campaign to win the confidence and adulation of the American public, a campaign geared for individuals such as the editor of a Virginia newspaper who wrote, "Any brave man would have walked down the aisle and arrested Dillinger. . . . Why were there so many cowards afraid of this one man? The answer is that the federal agents are mostly cowards."

This, then, was the task of the government—to convince the public that the hero was not Jesse or Butch or John Dillinger; the hero was the federal agent, fearless, educated, trained in the latest sophisticated methods of crime detection and enforcement, a selfless battler against injustice, a servant of the people against evil forces arrayed against him. Soon after Dillinger's last breaths, Hollywood was sending forth Jimmy Cagney in *The G-Man,* magazines and comic books and ten-cent pulp monthlies were extolling the Federal Bureau of Investigation, bubble gum cards were heralding the agents as "Heroes of the Law," their Thompsons blazing; and J. Edgar Hoover was entrenched in a seat of power. According to *The Feds,* one of the adventure magazines, the Director was "America's popular Public Hero No. 1."

By early 1935 nearly all of the major Hollywood studios were racing to produce pictures portraying the activities of the G-men. The studios, at the insistence of the Justice Department, were required to file stories, scripts, and titles for approval. When Paramount advised the department that it planned to release a film called *Federal Dicks,* Hoover was infuriated. "The agents of this Bureau are not 'Dicks,'" he fumed, "and

J. Edgar Hoover meets the press after the Dillinger killing, July 23, 1934. (National Archives, 65-H-98-6)

I think it is a most humiliating and repugnant title. . . . "

July 27, 1935 (almost exactly a year after Dillinger's death), NBC radio, coast-to-coast, Chevrolet Motor Company presenting the first of a series called "G-Men," written by Phillips H. Lord, made in cooperation with government officials, personally approved by Mr. Hoover: "Good evening. Chevrolet Motor Company is proud to announce tonight the opening of a series of dramatized broadcasts of vital interest and concern to every citizen of the United States. . . . Tonight, you will hear for the first time on the air a dramatic interpretation of the life and death of John Dillinger, bank robber, jailbreaker, and killer. . . . "

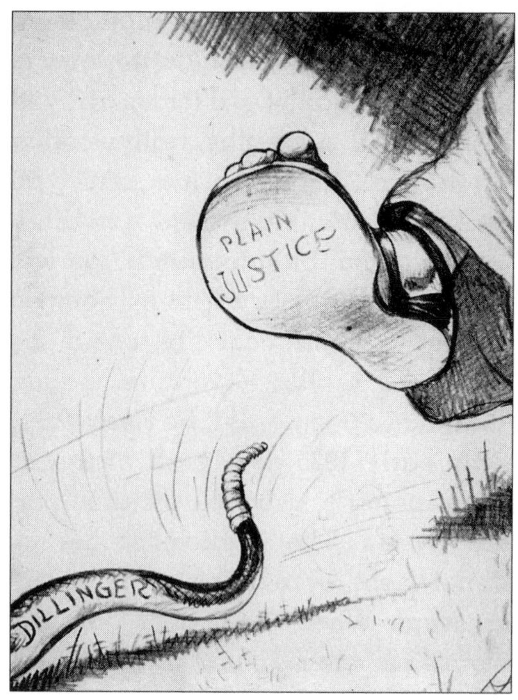

"Plain Justice" steps on Dillinger.

(National Archives, 65-HC-8-8)

A visitor to the offices of Hoover in the early 1940s would see in the anteroom a white plaster facsimile of Dillinger's death mask encased under glass. Surrounding the mask were other artifacts memorializing the showdown at the Biograph Theater, such items as the straw hat with a bullet hole through it, a snapshot of a girl friend that federal officers found in Dillinger's trousers, his broken eyeglasses, and a La-Corona-Belvedere cigar lifted from his shirt pocket. Some thought the museum-type exhibit macabre, especially in that office setting.

Decades later, Hoover would inevitably turn conversations

J. Edgar Hoover with friend and assistant Clyde Tolson at the Louis-Sharkey fight in August 1936.

(National Archives, 65-H-131-1)

Gary Cooper at the FBI, February 14, 1938.

(National Archives, 65-H-62)

back to the Dillinger case, back to that great victory that cemented his own fortunes and those of the agency he so personified. "Hoover had a thing about Dillinger," an FBI assistant director once said. Hoover called him "the flag-bear of lawlessness" and Dillinger became his trophy, like a grizzly or lion felled on an expedition. "The night we got John Dillinger our agents phoned me from Chicago that he had gone into a movie theater, and they were waiting for him to emerge. He was in there exactly two hours and four minutes—but as I sat, waiting at my home here, it seemed like a lifetime." The Indiana criminal had put himself center-stage

J. Edgar Hoover meets legendary cowboy actor Tom Mix.

(National Archives, 65-H-162-3)

J. Edgar Hoover worked with numerous movie greats to enhance the image of the FBI. Hoover meets with Edward G. Robinson at MGM studios in September 1937.

(National Archives, 65-H-215-4)

and was the focus of the greatest manhunt in American history. When the Feds brought him down they had won a battle of wits, a war of images, and, above all, a struggle for power.

If Dillinger had become the greatest trophy in J. Edgar Hoover's life of crime fighting, an icon around which he built a career, others in the law enforcement business had even

more personal memories of bringing in Dillinger. Out in Arizona, members of the Tucson police department remembered their own triumph. They had captured the elusive outlaw and several members of his gang. They had recovered stolen money and an arsenal of weapons and hadn't lost a life or taken one. They had brought a legend in alive without even a police radio system.

And from decade to decade the legend lives. Nashville, Indiana, 1975, a small town in Brown County, known mostly for its delicious apple butter. Two ex-lawmen, one a former FBI agent and the other a Pinkerton, open the John Dillinger Historical Wax Museum. Here, one finds carved figures not only of the Hoosier state's favorite bandit son, born forty-five miles north of here, but also other notable outlaws of his time—Ma Barker, Clyde Barrow, and Pretty Boy Floyd. Here, one finds the famous wooden gun, letters from Dillinger to his mother, family photos, his rabbit foot, and mug shots. One also finds a morgue room featuring the wicker casket in which Dillinger's body was carried from the Cook County morgue to the hearse on July 24, 1934, and an autopsy table on which another wax figure of the outlaw lies prone, bullet-pierced and bloodstained.

July 1984. Chicago's Biograph Theater marks a fifty-year anniversary of Dillinger's demise by playing *Manhattan Melodrama*. A thousand people line the street to join the festivities, including many men dressed in straw boaters and women wearing red.

January 1994. The Hotel Congress in downtown Tucson commemorates the sixtieth anniversary of Dillinger's cap-

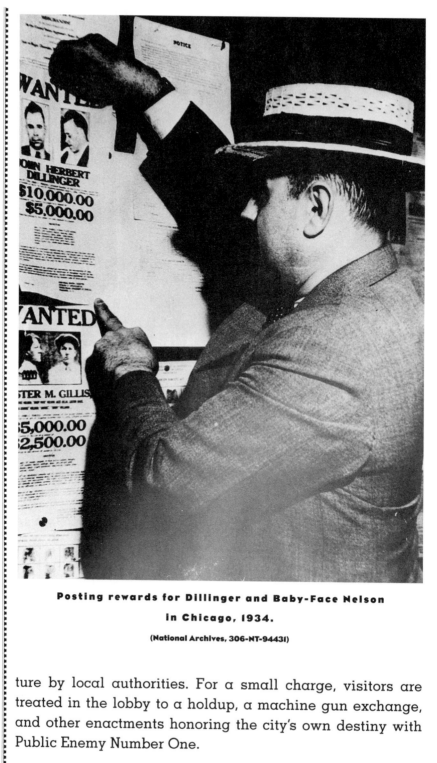

Posting rewards for Dillinger and Baby-Face Nelson in Chicago, 1934.

(National Archives, 306-NT-94431)

ture by local authorities. For a small charge, visitors are treated in the lobby to a holdup, a machine gun exchange, and other enactments honoring the city's own destiny with Public Enemy Number One.

12

Jesse and Charley

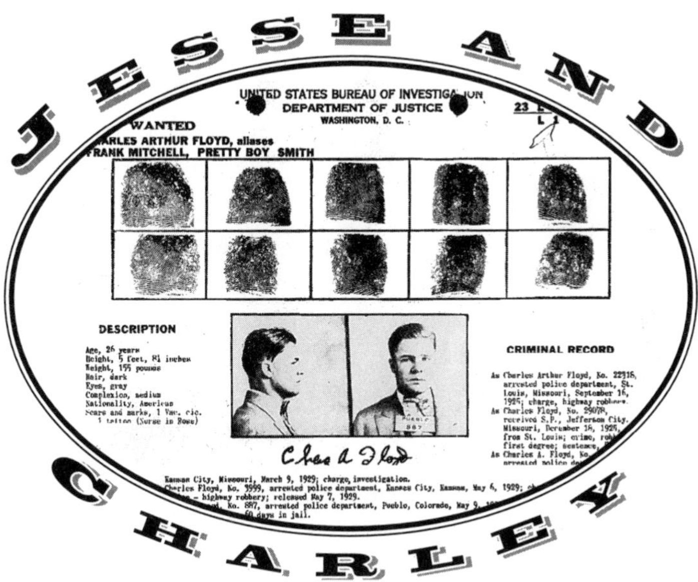

Pretty Boy Floyd wanted poster.

(National Archives, RG 60, DJ Classified Subject Files)

COME AND GATHER 'ROUND ME,

CHILDREN

A STORY I WILL TELL

ABOUT PRETTY BOY FLOYD, THE OUTLAW,

OKLAHOMA KNEW HIM WELL.

212

The ballad glorifies Oklahoma's most notorious folk bandit; the balladeer was Oklahoma's most celebrated writer of folk music. In March 1939, Woody Guthrie composed a song that melded the Robin Hood bandit folk myth with populist political vision. Here was outlaw Pretty Boy, misunderstood, a victim of circumstance, driven to a life of crime by poverty and fate, who, from backwoods hideouts amidst caverns and gullies, protected by country folk, preyed on the rich and their banks and their hired guns. In a time of social upheaval and dislocation, here was a romantic figure who could take back from the exploiters, the capitalist bankers and the railroad barons. Here was a man of brains and guts who had risen from rock bottom.

In return for the people's shelter and help, the outcast outlaw paid off mortgages, sent truckloads of groceries to families on relief, and left thousand-dollar bills on dinner tables after begging meals. To the farmers and hill people of

Oklahoma, Pretty Boy Floyd had made their fight against poverty and exploitation his own fight, had made their enemies his own.

NOW, AS THROUGH THIS WORLD I RAMBLE
I'VE SEEN LOTS OF FUNNY MEN
SOME WILL ROB YOU WITH A SIX-GUN
AND SOME WITH A FOUNTAIN PEN.

In an interview with folklorist Alan Lomax, Woody Guthrie later talked about his own hard times in Oklahoma, about being broke and sleeping in barns and about seeing Lincoln Zephyrs driven by drunk rich men hauling around women sporting expensive diamonds and necklaces. He would think then how one of those diamonds could buy a little farm with a good "water well and a gourd dipper and forty acres of good bottom land and some chickens to wake me up in the morning." When he would think about these things, Guthrie said, he would think about how a man like Charley Floyd could become a thief and yet a hero.

Many people of Oklahoma's eastern sand hill country, Woody said, hated banks and the fear of foreclosure; hated sheriffs and deputies, those hirelings of the rich; and they especially hated their own anonymity. A lot of those plain people, those solid people, said Woody, knew Charley Floyd personally.

THERE'S MANY A STARVING FARMER
THE SAME OLD STORY TOLD
HOW THIS OUTLAW PAID THEIR MORTGAGE
AND SAVED THEIR LITTLE HOME.

Woody's own Uncle Claude, according to the family story, was once hurt seriously while working in the oil fields near Seminole. As he tried to walk home, he fell along the road. A car stopped, picked him up, and rushed him to the hospital. The samaritan was Charley Floyd.

Many of the folktales about Floyd that flowed out of eastern Oklahoma were about such incidents, some of the tales grounded in actual events, others concocted from rich imagination and embellishment. Woody Guthrie not only respected the historical figure of Floyd but cherished the legend—about a man from the common people fighting against the entrenched interests and embarrassing them.

The outlaw legends of the earlier years, Jesse and Billy the Kid and Cole Younger, all inspired music, Woody said. "You hear songs about those fellers springing up everywhere like flowers in the right early spring." Oklahoma never had a governor half as popular as Pretty Boy, said Woody. "You couldn't come down in my part of Oklahoma and say nothing against him. If you did, something was liable to hit you, son, and it wouldn't be no train. . . . "

In 1941, Woody Guthrie wrote to some friends about visiting Oakie work camps on the West Coast and singing in tents and shacks and some government buildings. When he sang about Tom Joad or Pretty Boy in those tents and shacks, Woody said, the folks "just dam [*sic*] near tore" them down.

Charles Floyd was born in 1904 in the red clay farming area of the hollows and hills of northwest Georgia, near Folsom. He was the second son and fourth child of Walter Lee Floyd and Mamie Helena Echols Floyd, descendants of Georgia hill farmers whose lineage could be traced back through three centuries of Welsh farmers.

In 1911, the Floyd family, leaving behind their Georgia roots and their poverty for another start, sold off the house and livestock, carried off as many of their belongings as they could pack in sacks and baskets, and boarded a train. They eventually stopped in Sequoyah County in mideastern Oklahoma, close to the Arkansas border, near the little towns of Sallisaw and Akins. To the north was Brushy Mountain and the Cookson Hills; south lay Wild Horse Mountain. The Floyds scratched out a living raising cotton, corn, and sorghum.

Back in the Midwest, in Indianapolis, Indiana, John

Dillinger, a year older than Charley, had lost his mother and was under the care of his father and older sister. Back east, in Washington, D.C., John Edgar Hoover, age sixteen, made plans to go to George Washington University. He seemed to be a model son and promising student.

Charley Floyd absorbed the sounds and sights of Oklahoma; spent long, arduous hours in the fields; spent time at Cherokee Green Corn Stomp Dances, hayrides, and country picnics; worked alongside moonshiners ripening yellow brew in warm barrels; went to religious revival meetings, hog slaughterings, and barn raisings; met cowherders and Indians; and heard stories of western heroes and badmen. And no place in the United States spawned such a large number of outlaw tales as eastern Oklahoma.

Oklahoma had been a state only four years when Charley Floyd's family arrived. Here in the infamous Indian Territory, where the Cherokees and four other "Civilized Tribes" had landed half a century earlier after being forced from their ancestral lands in the East, Colonel William Quantrill's guerrillas had burned and looted. Here, the Daltons, the Youngers, the Doolin gang, and other bandits had robbed and killed and found refuge in the labyrinth of creeks and streams, in the bluffs and secluded oak-rich passes of the Ozark Mountain region. Here, Judge Isaac Parker, in Fort Smith, had cast assorted murderers, rustlers, and thieves to the scaffold to "hang by the neck until you are dead, dead, dead!" Charley Floyd heard the stories of deputy marshals turned criminal; but he also heard of the exploits of other lawmen who stayed honest, Bill Tilghman, Heck Thomas, and the others. He heard of quick-draw gunmen and sudden violence and immortal escapes.

But of all the legends, all the heroic figures of the West, one man alone far eclipsed the others in Charley Floyd's mind—Jesse. To the young Floyd, Jesse became an obsession. He listened to older farmers share insights about Jesse's forays into Indian Country, pestered his parents to buy dime novels about the exploits of the famed Missouri outlaw, and bought

Jesse's Robin Hood image totally. The daring, persecuted Jesse, driven by events and circumstances, hounded by sniveling bankers and their hired guns, faithful to his friends, his own kind—this was a man on whom to lavish awe and reverence. Floyd never tired of hearing the old stories of Jesse's making fools out of his enemies, and as Floyd got older those stories became more than sources of amusement; they became blueprints.

As the United States entered the world war in 1917, the latest branches of the Floyd family tree were now in Sequoyah County, Oklahoma. Brothers and sisters, uncles and aunts, and cousins dominated the area around Akins, a place called "Sweet Town," given that name because of all the sorghum molasses made there. The Floyd clan worked the backwoods and did all the other things common to tenant farmers.

But for Charley Floyd, restless and tired of the drudgery of farm life, this was not enough. With his cherubic face and his dark auburn hair combed straight back, Floyd charmed a succession of young women, drawn not only by his good looks but by his easy swagger and playful manner. Spending whatever spare time he had in the bars of nearby towns, Floyd swilled so much Choctaw beer that his friends began to call him "Chock."

Tough, stocky, at age sixteen he packed his grips and headed west, hopping freights, hitching rides in hay wagons and flivvers. He hired on with farmers in Oklahoma and Kansas, baled and raked hay, shucked corn, and threshed wheat. In Joplin he visited the bawdy houses and bars. Later, he landed in Wichita, the old cattle-shipping center that had years earlier attracted such Wild West figures as Bill Tilghman, Wyatt Earp, and Bat Masterson. Wichita had shed its cowboy days and had grown into a plains city of nearly eighty thousand people. It was in Wichita that Floyd met John Callahan.

Operating from a junkyard on the train tracks near Union Station, the white-haired Irishman managed one of the largest fencing operations in the Midwest. Bank robbers from all over the area, including bandit baron Frank Nash, made their way to the junkyard to trade stolen bonds for twenty cents on the dollar.

In the portly, pipe-smoking Callahan, Floyd had found his own link to the shadowy outlaw world that had driven his fantasies. Callahan knew crime; he knew its language, its methods, and its people. To Floyd, he became a mentor. As the youngster ran errands for the old-time Fagin, he met numerous crooks and ex-cons, some of whom had known such notorious outlaws as Al Spencer and Henry Starr. Back in Oklahoma, young Floyd had heard stories about Starr, and now in Kansas he had talked to men who had actually met the legend. When Floyd returned to Oklahoma and his family and friends, he was a man more focused.

In 1924 Chock Floyd married Ruby Hargrove, a farmer's daughter from the town of Bixby and they soon had a son named Jack Dempsey Floyd. For a time, Floyd stayed with his new family and with the farm life, working on the cotton crop and helping plant the seed corn. By 1925, however, he could stay no longer.

Without telling Ruby his plan, the restless Floyd traded five gallons of white lightning for a pearl-handled forty-four, hopped a freight with some friends, and headed east. A few days later, on September 11, 1925, three armed men robbed couriers in St. Louis of an $11,000 payroll bound for the Kroger Grocery and Baking Company. Witnesses said they could identify the robbers. On September 13, Chock and his friend arrived back in Sallisaw chomping on four-bit stogies, decked out in shiny suits and felt hats, and driving a new Studebaker roadster. Three days later, Floyd and his accomplice, charged with armed robbery and chained by their ankles and hands, were led onto a train for a ride back to St. Louis. Floyd soon entered the Missouri State Penitentiary in Jefferson City facing a five-year sentence—or, as inmates put it, "doing hard time on a nickel." He was prisoner number 29078.

Back in Oklahoma, a book titled *The Rise and Fall of Jesse James* was being serialized in the *Tulsa World.* And on the day Chock Floyd arrived in St. Louis as a prisoner, Douglass Starr, sixteen-year-old nephew of bank robber Henry Starr, was given a fifteen-year sentence for a robbery in Newkirk, Oklahoma. Less than a week earlier, Emmett Daugherty, another Henry Starr nephew, died near Bartlesville from a deputy sheriff's bullets. The next bandit legend from Oklahoma would not be a member of the Starr clan. The next bandit legend from Oklahoma was now in prison in Missouri learning new angles from seasoned veterans.

The new prisoner listened to veteran burglars explain techniques of blowing safes; he heard stories about evading police dragnets; he learned about the easiest banks to hit and the ones to avoid; he got tips on state and federal laws, on the latest weapons, on corruptible cops and judges, and on the best possible gang members available for hire. He stored away the tips and waited.

In Floyd's chosen line of work, these were propitious times. An editorialist for the *St. Paul Pioneer Press* lamented that "the United States is approaching a condition somewhat resembling anarchy . . . " A writer for the *Chicago Evening News* joined the chorus: "The increasing complexities of our modern civilization and the decreasing efficiency of those restraints which were once found in the home and religion are factors tending to the making of criminals."

Headlines screamed of murder, robbery, bootlegging, arson, and kidnapping; of lawlessness in big cities; of vigilance committees; of a country in economic decline and under a rising tide of gangsterism. A Chicago judge called it "armed insurrection." The homicide rate in New York and Chicago reached about one a day. At the same time, in all of England and Wales, there were less than two hundred killings a year. Philosophers and pundits mused about the causes: hard times, frontier morals, the coddling of crooks, the triumph of the Devil, too many guns. The *Boston Globe* pointed out that Americans carried more revolvers than all of the people of Europe and Asia combined. *Scribner's* blamed the whole sordid mess on the nation's glorification of the criminal, the hero-worship of thugs and murderers, those dreadful dime novels that turned kids' minds, and those movies that romanticized ne'er-do-wells such as Jesse.

On January 4, 1929, Ruby Floyd filed for divorce, charging neglect. Charley did not contest it, and Ruby took custody of the four-year-old Dempsey. Over the years, Floyd continued to see his former wife and son; indeed, the three of them lived together for a time in Tulsa. In March 1929 Charley Floyd walked out of Jefferson City pen. He was free, now, to make a new start, to get his life together.

On May 6, 1929, Floyd was picked up by Kansas City police and jailed on suspicion of highway robbery, booked, given another mug shot and another number. This was not an auspicious beginning for the next bandit hero. The next day Floyd was back on the street. It had all been a mistake. He headed west. Two days later he was in jail again, this time in Pueblo, Colorado, arrested for vagrancy. He was fined $50 and served several weeks. A few weeks later, Kansas City authorities brought him in on suspicion of robbing a Sears Roebuck plant. Within a few months after he had walked out of Jefferson City, Floyd had been jailed three times. And he apparently hadn't made an illegal nickel. It could have been the looks, that shining, dark hair swept back by sweet-smelling pomade, slick as axle grease, that big bow tie, that swagger, those shirtsleeves rolled up revealing that new tattoo on the inside of his left arm, a tattoo of a rose with the image of a Red Cross nurse inside the rose's petal. To many, the man looked suspicious.

To others, he looked sexy. To nineteen-year-old Beulah Baird, a bobbed-haired beauty at Mother Ash's boardinghouse in Kansas City, he not only looked sexy, he looked like a "pretty boy." The moniker, of course, stuck, although Floyd at times seemed embarrassed by it. A whole mythology later grew about the "pretty boy" appellation—he got it from a famous madam at a whorehouse in Kansas City; he got it from friends in the Cookson Hills; he got it from a paymaster present at the Kroger Grocery heist. But according to Chock Floyd himself, he got it from Beulah Baird.

"Pretty Boy" Floyd. Now this was a character for the reporters. He had the brains, the knowledge, the desire, the image. He now had to deliver the goods. FBI agent Melvin Purvis wrote: "Floyd was handsome in a heavy-browed, defiant fashion; and he was possessed by a queer and fatalistic sort of vanity. He was fully convinced that his life was destined to be short and that he would die violently."

For a while, he dabbled in bootleg enterprises. Congregating with other ex-cons from Jefferson City, he roamed the Kansas City tenderloins looking for action from the hoods and the hookers. Things in Kansas City were there for the taking, Floyd could see, and most everyone, including the police, was on the take.

Early in 1930, Floyd joined some older ex-cons from Jefferson City, added some other gentlemen with solid bank-robbing credentials, and completed the team with a woman shoplifter from Kansas City who agreed to cook for the boys. Setting up headquarters in a small cottage in an isolated section of the country's tire capital, Akron, Ohio, the gang plotted a series of hits in northern Ohio.

On February 5, 1930, the infant gang rolled a Studebaker sedan into Sylvania, Ohio, near Toledo. The target: Farmers & Merchants Bank. Armed with a double-action Smith & Wesson .32, Floyd, with three accomplices, charged through the door, rounded up the noonday customers, and lined them up against the wall. He asked the cashier to open the massive vault door. Informed that the vault had a time lock that would not open for another five hours, Floyd became upset. One of the frustrated bandits knocked the cashier to the floor with a blow to the skull. More frustration ensued. When the gang had lined their captives against the bank wall, a worker at a gas station across the street noticed the peculiar scene and called the fire department. With the sounding of the fire alarm, the bandits grabbed a few bucks out of the tellers' cash drawers, backed out into the street, climbed into the Studebaker, and sped away. They were closely followed by a fire truck, lights flashing, siren screaming, driven by the town fire chief, accompanied by his assistant fire chief, who had grabbed a shotgun. Down the streets of Sylvania roared the five robbers followed by the fire truck, with the assistant fire chief leaning out the window, anxious to get a shot. The truck was now going at its top speed. Eventually, the getaway car prevailed in the chase by weaving in and out of traffic situations the truck could not negotiate. Although the gang escaped, members of the Sylvania town fire department began to tell tales that evening of their own deeds of raw heroism, tales that would be passed on to future generations of this small Ohio town.

For Floyd, this was still not anything like Jesse; it was embarrassing. And things kept getting worse. Acting on a tip from a mission house preacher who had learned some information about the hideout from a tramp, Akron police raided the place, found the gang, beat them up, and booked them. In the aftermath of the violent skirmish, a police officer died.

Although the subsequent investigation in Ohio proved that Floyd had not committed murder, he was charged with armed robbery in the assault on the Sylvania bank. Back in jail, this time in Toledo, Pretty Boy glumly contemplated his future. On November 10, 1930, in the Ohio State Penitentiary in Columbus, James Bradley, the member of the Floyd gang who had killed the police officer in Akron, was led to the electric chair. Reportedly, he quipped to one of the guards, "I'm due for a shocking this evening."

A month later, the Ohio State Penitentiary made preparations to welcome another guest. Accompanied by several detectives, Floyd boarded a New York Central train in Toledo for a ride from jail to the penitentiary. Near Kenton, Ohio, along the Scioto River, he managed to break out a window in a bathroom and leap down a steep embankment. Instead of running, he hid among some thick weeds as detectives and members of the train crew fanned out in the dark, cold night.

The pursuers had been hoodwinked. From the time of this escape in Ohio, Floyd would never again be in handcuffs, would never again be booked. This, now, was more like Jesse.

Hitching rides through back roads from Ohio to Illinois, Floyd picked his way west, past small towns and ambitious sheriffs who could have made their reputations by taking in the fugitive. For Floyd, it was now back to Kansas City, back to the whorehouses and the bars and pool halls, back to the gamblers, bootleggers, drug dealers, and bandits, the society in which this player would rapidly become a grand master.

Floyd found a new partner, Willis Miller, better known as "Billy the Killer." Willis had earned the moniker by killing his own brother in a duel at Hell's Half Acre, a bootlegger hide-out near East Liverpool, Ohio. In the spring of 1930, the two robbed banks in Arkansas and Kentucky. In sleepy Bowling Green, Kentucky, the two dapper thieves faced off against the chief of police and a deputy in a raucous gunfight that made national wire stories. Floyd got away; Miller, along with the deputy, died. Wood County prosecutor Raymond Ladd issued a charge of first-degree murder against Charles Arthur Floyd. He was the target of a manhunt, now, worth a bounty of a thousand bucks. Prohibition agents, sheriffs, deputies, and rookie cops all knew the face and knew the reputation.

In Kansas City, on July 20, 1931, the stakes rose. At a liquor warehouse on the north side of the city, above a flower shop, Floyd was cornered with some other men by federal agents. Streams of gunfire slashed into whiskey bottles and bodies. Five men crumpled with assorted wounds. One of the agents later died. Floyd, in the middle of it all, escaped unharmed. His bounty price increased.

WANTED

FOR BANK ROBBERY AND MURDER

CHARLES ARTHUR FLOYD (PRETTY BOY).

AGE 27 YEARS; 5 FEET, 8 1/2 INCHES TALL;

WEIGHT 170 POUNDS; MUSCULAR BUILD; MEDIUM COMPLEXION; GREY EYES; VACCINATION SCAR ON LEFT ARM; TATTOO OF RED CROSS NURSE ON LEFT ARM.

The rabbit returned to the briar patch; Floyd returned to Oklahoma. Here in the Cookson Hills, he found refuge in familiar terrain and familiar faces, found time to regain strength. He told some friends that the bandit business was exhausting. Sometimes, he said, he felt like an old man.

By late 1931, Floyd had still another new partner. Part Cherokee, part Choctaw, part Irish, George Birdwell, with his cowboy boots and Stetson, with women at his call, seemed a likely Floyd buddy. Like Floyd he had swagger and cockiness and imagination. The two launched a partnership that lasted nearly two years, through several Oklahoma bank jobs, from Earlsboro, Shamrock, and Morris to Maud, Earlsboro, and Castle, a town seven miles northwest of Okemah, the birthplace of Woody Guthrie.

Wielding submachine guns and revolvers, steel chest protectors under their expensive suits, shoes spit-shined, Floyd and company struck in broad daylight just as the old-time bandit heroes had done. Floyd joked and chatted with bank employees and avoided strong-armed force; the image was as important as the take. He passed out money to family and friends, paid for meals when on the run, did everything he could to curry favor with the citizenry. He carried around a copy of *When the Daltons Rode,* a memoir penned by aging Emmett Dalton and published in 1931 by Doubleday. According to Floyd's relatives, the book on the Daltons, just like the books on Jesse, was an inspiration and guide. "An outlaw's got to be cagey as a coyote," the book taught. "The alert outlaw acts a good deal by intuition. His wits and senses become acute as a wild animal's."

With rewards posted, with stories about Pretty Boy in the press in several states, with rumors abundant, the myth-making rolled on. Suddenly, Floyd was everywhere. People sighted him in tourist camps, in cafés, on the highways, and at the scenes of myriad crimes. Suddenly, unsolved crimes in state after state were attributed to Floyd, as were imaginative quotes, some fanciful, some real. He did say in a letter, "I have robbed no one but the monied men." Suddenly, this quote was in articles across the country with apt comparisons with Robin Hood.

Law enforcement officials, bristling with contempt for the notoriety of this uncommon thief and the unfavorable remarks about his ingenuity compared with their own, reacted predictably. They promised to Swiss cheese the man. Bankers, embarrassed by the robberies, infuriated by the loss of money, insulted by comparisons in the press between the outlaw's generosity and their own penuriousness, also reacted predictably. Eugene Gum, secretary of the Oklahoma Bankers' Association, declared in words as passionate as they were logic-defying: "He is the sort of criminal who must be killed before he is captured." Walter Biscup, editorial writer for the *Tulsa World,* waxed dramatic: "With a submachine gun nestling in the crook of his left arm and purring an uncontrollable message of sudden death to its objectives, he is acting his part with a macabre flair of seriousness." Charley Floyd, said Biscup, was making the legendary Henry Starr and other homicidal bandits insignificant footnotes in the history of western outlawry. In Oklahoma City, a newsboy stood on a street corner barking out the afternoon edition: "Read all about it! Officers escape from Pretty Boy Floyd! Officers escape from Pretty Boy Floyd!"

On April 9, 1932, a longtime Oklahoma lawman named Erv Kelley, who had been trailing Floyd for three months, ambushed the bandit near Bixby. In a submachine gun shootout, Kelley died. The heat on Floyd now reached feverish dimensions. Huge posses of state officers assembled their arsenals and took to the Oklahoma back roads. They even brought in famed aviator Wiley Post, who directed aerial surveillance, circling the hills where the outlaw lurked in his lair. Rewards encouraged extermination: to shoot down

Floyd in Oklahoma would now bring five times the reward for bringing him in alive.

On November 1, 1932, a week before the national election that ushered in the era of Franklin Roosevelt, Floyd and George Birdwell and a young kid they had hired as a driver pulled off the kind of audacious stunt on which bandit lore voraciously fed. Floyd decided to rob the State Bank in Sallisaw, his hometown. As the Ford sedan rolled slowly into Sallisaw at noontime, Floyd waved to a few friends on the street. This was one bank job in which the bandits sought eyewitnesses; Floyd was performing for the home folks. Stepping from the car directly in front of the bank, he lodged his submachine gun under his left arm, gazed up and down the street at the many townspeople who stood entranced. He talked briefly with the town barber, saluted other friends, and marched into the bank to carry out perhaps the easiest robbery in history. The chief of police sat in his car less than a hundred yards away from the scene. Asked later about his indifference, he claimed that he was totally oblivious to the event.

When the citizens of Sallisaw watched Floyd, cocksure and confident, take money from the town bank, many were enjoying a vicarious victory—and Floyd knew it. If the Depression had robbed men of jobs, if bankers had robbed them of money and land, this adopted son of the Oklahoma hill folk had shown grit and guts, and they cheered him on. A reporter who made his way to Sallisaw later described the event as like "the hometown performance of a great actor who has made it good on Broadway."

To track Floyd in the Cookson Hills was a source of great frustration. As officers visited farm after farm attempting to elicit information on the fugitive, men and women would inevitably claim total ignorance of his whereabouts; head after head would shake negatively to questions about his movements. It was as if the hill country grapevine was electrically charged, sending out messages to all points when agents entered the region. The trail always disappeared into the vast, jutting mountains, into the caves and caverns. An Oklahoma Bankers' Association official was dubious about the possibility of finding Floyd in the hills: "Too much home folks," he lamented.

In November 1932, Charley lost another partner. George Birdwell, foolishly acting on his own, tried to rob a bank in Boley, Oklahoma, a town settled entirely by blacks after the Civil War. Law enforcement officials and the Oklahoma Bankers' Association did not mourn Bird's loss along with Floyd. OBA Secretary Gum echoed his earlier sentiments: "The remedy is to kill them. Don't ask them to surrender."

The swinging door of a speakeasy in the hills flies open and three men amble inside carrying guns. The leader declares, "You all know who I am. Now back up against the wall and let us do some drinking." No one challenged him, even though rewards were inviting. No one later ran to the law or raced to a telephone. Instead, they quietly left, fortified with a great story they would retell for years. They had drunk with Pretty Boy.

In early 1933, Floyd innocently became a suspect in the killing of two police officers near Columbia, Missouri, and the manhunt became even more frantic. Politicians; law enforcement officials—state, local, and federal; civic leaders; editorialists—all called for Floyd's death. For the fugitive, the chase was exciting but exhausting. Every chance encounter on the road, every strange face in a restaurant, every gas station attendant, every glimpse of a car or sound of a siren, every flirtation could signal trouble. He was now wanted for far more crimes than he had committed, even some that had occurred at the same time in far different locations. And now, in June 1933, Floyd became the chief suspect in a massacre.

In 1924, Frank "Jelly" Nash, a veteran Oklahoma bandit, bootlegger, and murderer, hooked up with outlaw Al Spencer in attempting to hit a mail train near Okesa, Oklahoma. He was caught and sent to Leavenworth. Six years later, working as a cook in the warden's residence, he walked out the back door with a three-volume edition of Shakespeare under his arm. Frank Nash also had some class.

By 1931 Nash had joined Alvin Karpis and the Barker gang in several holdups, fled to Kansas City, and spent much time playing golf with assorted crime characters such as Francis Keating, Thomas Holden, and kidnapper Harvey Bailey. The fugitives moved between the criminal havens of St. Paul, Chicago, Kansas City, and their favorite nineteenth hole, Hot Springs, Arkansas, the spa oasis for the underworld.

When Keating and Holden were apprehended on the Old Mission Golf Course in Hot Springs by Justice Department agents, Jelly Nash felt the heat. He contracted the services of a surgeon to straighten his crooked nose and purchased a toupee. Using the alias "Doc Williams," Nash planned to lay low in Hot Springs, gambling, visiting the whorehouses, and soaking up the thermal waters on Bathhouse Row, protected by a friendly and well-paid-off police department. But federal agents, unimpressed with the attempted disguise, tracked the wily crook and caught him in front of the White Front Pool Hall, a race booking joint owned by a bunco and con artist named Richard Galatas, a friend of the Hot Springs mayor and chief of police.

The agents hustled their captive into a car and headed north. Word of the abduction, witnessed by a few members of Nash's criminal society, sped north faster than the agents, and much of the underworld knew of Nash's predicament. At Fort Smith, Arkansas, the agents loaded Nash into a Missouri Pacific train bound for Kansas City. J. Edgar Hoover wired instructions that the prisoner be taken from Kansas City to the federal penitentiary at Leavenworth, Kansas.

On the morning of Saturday, June 17, 1933, the train rolled into Union Station, and the agents, now accompanied by several Kansas City policemen, marched Nash out of the station and into the parking lot of the outdoor plaza, where a Chevy sedan waited to haul the prisoner off to the penitentiary. In the mind of Frank Smith, a Department of Justice agent from Oklahoma City, the next few seconds would be powerfully

Two of the country's greatest crime warriors—Attorney General Homer Cummings and FBI agent Melvin Purvis.

(National Archives, 306-NT-94981)

burned: "We all walked through the Union Station with Frank Nash still handcuffed. Nash was the first to enter the car which was to take us to the Leavenworth prison. He started to sit down in the rear seat. Someone told him he was to ride in front. So Nash sat down temporarily in the driver's seat while we were getting into the rear . . . I heard a man shouting, 'Up, up!' The words came fast. I reached for my six-shooter, drew it, and then looked up in time to see a man aiming a machine gun. It was shooting red flame. I don't know what all happened. I ducked as bullets splintered our car. I crouched down and played dead. It was the only thing that could be done."

Several men who had driven into the parking lot in a Reo sedan blasted a spray of bullets into the car with Nash and the agents. Within seconds, the parking lot was wild with panic and confusion; with bullets zipping into cars, into walls, and into bodies; with station porters running, men in business suits rolling to the ground for cover, and children looking around quizzically, their parents terrified. Nash lay lifeless, instantly killed by the fusillade. Four other bodies sprawled in grotesque poses among the cars.

It didn't take the Justice Department long to finger their prime suspect—Pretty Boy Floyd. Floyd had been in Kansas City at the time of the shooting. A few prodded witnesses thought they might have recognized him.

For sixty years after those few seconds at Union Station, the Kansas City Massacre has been featured in articles, movies, fiction, and historical accounts. Many times, Floyd has been judged guilty. He was not. This was not Charley Floyd's style. Hit-and-run bank jobs, crime with flair and daring, a reluctance to engage in violence—these had marked his career. Floyd was not a hired gun or an assassin; indeed, such an act as that perpetrated in Kansas City would have been a rejection of the careful image he had gone to such detail and energy to create. Besides, this job had nothing to do with making money or cultivating image. Floyd vehemently denied to his relatives and friends that he had anything to do with the slaughter—and, as one family member said, Charley never refused to tell those folks anything.

Despite intensive probing, Hoover was never able to link Floyd with the crime. Internal FBI memoranda shortly after the event reveal no evidence connecting Floyd. Gangsters

Vern Miller, Walter Underhill, and Robert Brady, the likely triggermen, all perished before the legal system could do its work. Miller was found dead in late November near Detroit, apparently a torture victim of the mob. Underhill was killed by federal agents in Oklahoma while resisting arrest, and Brady was killed by local police officers near Paola, Kansas.

Despite the fact that Floyd was not a likely participant in the massacre, Hoover used the event to stir the public and other lawmen across the country to stop at nothing to bring down the infamous bandit. The Kansas City shootout made Floyd's annihilation almost certain. He would never be brought in alive.

An army mobilized in the Cookson Hills. Three companies of the Oklahoma National Guard, called up by Governor William Murray, blocked roads throughout the region while Guard companies in adjacent counties stood ready for duty. Federal agents, military officers, local police officers, sheriffs, and Guardsmen fanned across eastern Oklahoma like a massive foxhunting party. They searched farms, limestone caverns, and the dense hills; they talked with thousands of farmers and mountain folk and townspeople and friends, relatives, and acquaintances of the notorious outlaw; they stretched their net taut. They came up with nothing. But the massive effort impressed Pretty Boy. He headed east.

Upholding his lofty credentials throughout the early months of 1934, Floyd struck banks in Iowa, Ohio, and Oklahoma, and some of his escapes were as slick as the pomade in his hair. But Charley knew that the streak would run out.

FBI agent Melvin Purvis, the man who had engineered the Dillinger manhunt, now homed in on Floyd. When Adam Richetti was picked up near Wellsville, Ohio, police discovered that Floyd had been with him a short time before. The Feds swooped in from Pittsburgh, Louisville, and Detroit, establishing a manhunt headquarters at the Travelers Hotel in East Liverpool, a small Ohio steel town. The agents checked doctors, hospitals, rental car establishments, taxi

J. Edgar Hoover and Melvin Purvis in 1934.

(National Archives, 65-H-123-1)

With Dillinger, Floyd, and others eliminated, "Law and Order" reigns

(National Archives, RG 60, DJ Classified Subject Files)

companies, hot dog stands, and garages. They posted sentinels at the bridges crossing the Ohio River. They stopped citizens along the roads to show them Floyd's picture. They interviewed Richetti's relatives and friends, took an increasing number of telephone calls from citizens who had now suddenly sighted Floyd, and chased down lead after lead.

Finally, on October 22, 1934, a farmer reported that he had just given some food to a man fitting the description of Floyd. In a lonely farm area near Youngstown, the manhunt ended. They shot him in the back.

For the dirty little coward
That shot Mr. Howard
Has laid poor Jesse in his grave.

The *New York Times* declared that the government had finished off "the most dangerous man alive." Hoover said his department had wiped out "a yellow rat who needed extinction."

Hoover quickly got the word out to reporters and writers. He wrote to Fulton Oursler, editor and chief of *Liberty Magazine:* "On the afternoon of October 22, 1934, a squad of Special Agents of the Division, accompanied by members of the East Liverpool, Ohio, Police Department, were cruising about the country making inquiries, and in response to these inquiries it was learned that an individual resembling Floyd had been seen in the neighborhood of the Bell Schoolhouse, and upon proceeding to that point an individual fitting the description of Floyd was observed on the farm of Mrs. Ellen Conkle. As they approached the farm this individual started to run across the field and was challenged to halt. Upon his failure to do so he was fired upon and mortally wounded, dying shortly thereafter. Before dying he identified himself as 'Pretty Boy Floyd,' which identification was later positively corroborated through examination and comparison of fingerprints."

On October 28, 1934, at Akins Cemetery in the Cookson Hills, the Floyd family and friends attended the funeral of Charley Floyd. So did twenty thousand other people. From Sallisaw and Vian and Gore and other towns in the hill country, and from towns and cities in over twenty states—including Ohio, where he died—people gathered to pay tribute. Six thousand automobiles, by police estimate—as well as wagons, trucks, buses, buggies, and horses—filled surrounding fields and hundreds more lined the highways and roads. The dust kicked loose by their tires, wheels, and hooves fed a heavy pea soup fog that settled over the area. Merchants reported a rousing sale of lunch meats, cheese, cookies, and fruit.

After a simple service featuring a sermon by the Reverend W. E. Rockett, pastor of the First Baptist Church, and songs by the Akins choir, the casket of the outlaw was opened so that the thousands could pay their respects. Many mourners packed pistols and carried corn liquor. Floyd's mother wept in the arms of Mrs. George Birdwell, widow of Charley's henchman who had been killed earlier. Floyd's nine-year-old son, according to many witnesses, bore a remarkable resemblance to his father.

Police officers from all over Oklahoma came to the funeral saturnalia. Many had vainly chased Floyd for nearly a decade and, for most, this was their first glimpse of the man. People collected rocks and tree leaves as souvenirs of the occasion. Hill folk with large boots and ten-gallon hats mingled with newspaper reporters and Indians and curiosity seekers in business clothes. Years later people still named their children after the legendary outlaw.

The poor kid from a dirt farm in dust bowl Oklahoma, the unschooled tough who had spent many nights of his youth in local saloons drinking Choctaw beer and carousing with frontier drifters and trollops, had seen himself going nowhere but to oblivion. But Jesse's road had beckoned and he had followed the example, and many of the farmers and backwoods folk of the Southwest had called him "The Robin Hood of the Cookson Hills."

As he collected information for the book that would become *Grapes of Wrath,* John Steinbeck personally interviewed dust bowl refugees from Oklahoma and also consulted documents produced by Federal Writers Project workers who also interviewed farmers and hill folk. When Ma and Pa

A billboard heralds the opening of *You Can't Get Away With It*, a film in which J. Edgar Hoover made a personal appearance.

(National Archives, 65-H-252-2)

Joad reminisce about Pretty Boy Floyd, they speak of a kid provoked to crime, a kid no worse in mind and character than those who killed him. Ma and Pa Joad were the real voices of the hill people of Oklahoma.

Pa Joad spoke for the back country people: "When Floyd was loose and goin' wild, law said we got to give him up—an' nobody give him up. Sometimes a fella got to sift the law." They sifted the law because Floyd, they said, was one of their own, because they remembered how he tore up first mortgages in banks he robbed, hoping the mortgages had not been recorded and that homesteaders could not be foreclosed. He rolled so many banks in Oklahoma in the early 1930s, they said, that bank insurance rates in the state doubled. He had no apologies: "I have robbed no one but moneyed men."

Hoover trumpeted the killing of Floyd as another triumph of law and justice over anarchy and national disgrace. The G-man, he knew, was the real hero, not the likes of Dillinger and Floyd. But legends surrounding Jesse and Butch and Pretty Boy and others would not be punctured by Hoover or the FBI. The bandit folk hero was too stolid a creation, was too rooted in American myth.

* * * * * * *

In 1960, nearly three decades after the rubout in the Ohio cornfield, there was Floyd on the big screen, a "sagebrush Robin Hood," according to the movie press clippings. There was handsome actor John Ericson carefully combing back his dark hair, telling his partner that he does not rob bank clerks who have holes in their shoes. After all, as everyone knows, Pretty Boy Floyd robs only moneyed men.

13

BANDIT HEROES

The Boot Hill of the 1930s with Bonnie and Clyde, Dillinger, and other lawbreakers.

(National Archives, 65-HC-7-43)

ON THE RUN FROM FEDERAL AND STATE AUTHORITIES, ALVIN KARPIS DECIDED ON A GRAND GESTURE TO POSTERITY, A PERSONAL TESTIMONY TO HIS FOREBEARS; HE PLANNED TO ROB A TRAIN, JUST LIKE THEY DID IN THE GREAT DAYS ON THE FRONTIER.

Old Ben Grayson, a veteran bank robber recently released from prison, was one of the first to hear of Karpis's plan. He was dubious. "Who the hell robs a train in this day and age?" old Ben asked quizzically. Later Karpis wrote, "I thought of the great bandits of the old West, the James brothers, the Dalton boys, and all the rest of them. They knocked over trains and I was going to pull the same stunt."

He did. On the afternoon of November 7, 1935, five well-dressed men carrying machine guns boarded an Erie Railroad train at a station in Garrettsville, Ohio, east of Cleveland, and made off in a Plymouth sedan with nearly $45,000. The *Evening Record and Daily-Courier Tribune* of Ravenna, Ohio, called the holdup the most exciting event that had ever occurred in Garrettsville: "Quickly, but with cool precision, two of the robber crew, in modern Jesse James style, lined the dozen odd bystanders against the east side of the depot, commanding them to keep their hands above their heads." Mrs. W. W. Thomas, wife of a Garrettsville physician, was standing in her garden across the street from the depot. "It happened just like a movie," she declared. "I couldn't believe my eyes."

A few weeks later, from a hideout in Paris, Texas, owned by the brother of Grace Goldstein, a prominent madam of the Southwest, Karpis complained that he had not scored big-time; he had wanted a take of several hundred thousand. But he consoled himself with the thought that he had, indeed, pulled off a robbery "just like the famous old Western bandits." Other newspapers obligingly compared him to Jesse. Karpis was pleased.

From Jesse to Dillinger to Pretty Boy Floyd to Alvin Karpis, the bandit legends thrived on notoriety. They lived for the feature article, fed on the public appetite for excitement and color.

They were all made larger than life by various mythmaking agents—novelists, newspaper reporters, movies, poets, folk song writers. The deeds of Jesse, Cole Younger, Sam Bass, and Pretty Boy were all honored in song; many became film heroes; all of them became the subject of countless articles, novels, and even cigar and bubble gum cards. With each new treatment on film, in song, and in print, the dimensions of the characters grew larger, the deeds more astounding, the motives more lofty, and the talents more extraordinary. In the 1930s, when J. Edgar Hoover sought to strengthen the power and image of the FBI and of himself and to crush the image of the bandit folk hero, he turned to the tools by which the bandit images had been created. He managed the news, he helped authors promote the deeds of lawmen, and he helped make movies. No longer would G-men be dupes or bunglers but heroic figures.

The bandits evoked the symbols of masculinity so powerful in cultural heroic myths—to be tough; to be battlers, conquerors at long odds, figures of muscle and steady nerves, able to exude courage, self-reliance; to exact physical revenge for wrongs committed; to display the grit of making it in a society plagued with traps and snares; to defend personal rights against corruption. From Jesse to Floyd, the bandit folk heroes took on qualities of guile and daring equal to great mythical heroes. Defiant, swaggering, rebellious, they taunted authority, defied danger, made foolish those armed against them.

Elements of the Robin Hood myth surrounded their lives. They were victims of injustice or fate, men transformed by circumstance into noble robbers who took from the wealthy and gave to the poor. Bill Miner, "The Grey Fox," assured all that he "robbed only corporations." Pretty Boy Floyd robbed only "moneyed men." Even though most of the stories of bandit generosity and nobility rested on anecdotal veneer, they fed well the heroic myth.

As do heroes from all cultures, the bandits escaped death. It was impossible that Jesse James had been conquered. As late as 1946, a man with the appropriate name of J. Frank Dalton convinced many Americans that he was the aged Jesse and that another man was in Jesse's grave. A noted crime historian claims that John Dillinger outwitted the FBI and the world and did not perish in a Chicago alley in 1934, that the body displayed in photographs in newspapers around the world was that of another man. The investigations into the deaths of Butch Cassidy and the Sundance Kid continue.

Finally, the bandits cultivated the support of local populations, from which they received food, supplies, refuge, and alibis. They did it from a combination of friendship, intimidation, and admiration. Jesse, the ex-Confederate guerrilla, continued to enjoy the support of Yankee-hating Missourians and others who saw in his outlaw success continued Southern resistance and a vicarious satisfaction in paying back the Federals. Pretty Boy found succor and safety in the Cookson Hill communities of eastern Oklahoma as the local boy who heaped embarrassment upon the hated banking and railroad interests. The Youngers, the Daltons, Sam Bass, Bill Doolin, and John Dillinger—all built a body of sympathizers among the citizenry, a body that acted as shield and supporter.

All these elements—the quest for notoriety, the Robin Hood identification, the evocation of masculine symbolism, the portrayal by mythmakers, the immortality, the popular support by segments of the population—served to create and sustain the American bandit hero. From the days of the six-shooter and swift horses to the era of the Thompson machine guns and Tin Lizzies, roving gangs of thieves rampaged across the country, terrorizing civic institutions and mocking law enforcement. They carried on their own little wars with American institutions and authorities. They excited and frightened the public; inspired decades of lurid headlines, poetry, novels, and folk songs; became the center of a national debate on crime and its consequences; and jarred the American government into changing the dimensions of federal police authority.

In the film *Butch Cassidy and the Sundance Kid,* one of the Wild Bunch outlaws, Bill "News" Carver, says to his leader, "I love reading my name in the newspapers, Butch." Bandits loved reading about bandits. So do we, News.

Notes on Sources

The principal manuscript sources consulted in the preparation of *The Bandit Kings* are the massive files of the Justice Department (in the custody of the National Archives) and records at the Federal Bureau of Investigation. In these materials is a wealth of information, much of it formerly classified—internal memos, orders between operatives in Washington and in the field, newspaper clippings, speeches, telegrams, interviews, court testimony, and letters from newspaper editors, informers, police officials, witnesses to crimes, even psychics and fortune-tellers. There are in these federal files absorbing documents that tell much about the complex stories of the bandit gangs, about the legends surrounding their exploits, and about the lawmen who tracked them down.

At the National Archives, the records of the Department of Justice (Record Group 60) cover the entire chronological sweep of the book, from early letters of marshals in isolated areas of the West to files relating to the Roosevelt administration's war on crime in the 1930s. At the FBI are case files on the Barkers, Karpis, Bonnie and Clyde, Dillinger, Floyd, Baby-Face Nelson, and other crime figures; papers of Hoover and Purvis and other FBI officials and agents; as well as other departmental materials relating to the various cases.

The book makes much use of newspaper coverage from towns and cities in various states. Many of the newspapers are on microfilm at the Library of Congress. A clipping file on the Dillinger capture is in the Arizona Historical Society in Tucson. The microfilm of the *Evening Record and Daily-Courier Tribune* is in the Ravenna, Ohio, public library.

The bibliography that follows lists articles and books consulted in the writing of the work.

Adams, James Truslow. "Why We Glorify Our Gangsters," *New York Times* (December 13, 1931).

Adams, Ramon. *Burs Under the Saddle: A Second Look at Books and Histories of the West.* Norman, Okla.: University of Oklahoma Press, 1964.

Allen, Henry. "Hoover: In an "Age of Heroes, We Made Him One; Now We're Rooting for the Villain," *Washington Post* (March 23, 1993).

Ayres, B. Drummund. "In Frank and Jesse James Country, the Passage of Time Finds a Town Ready to Forgive—And Cash In," *New York Times* (April 5, 1972).

Baker, Pearl. *The Wild Bunch at Robbers Roost.* Lincoln: The University of Nebraska Press, 1965.

Ball, Larry D. "Frontier Sheriffs at Work," *Journal of Arizona History* (Autumn 1986), 283–296.

———. "Just and Right in Every Particular: U.S. Marshal Zan Tidball and the Politics of Frontier Law Enforcement," *Journal of Arizona History* (Summer 1993).

———. "Lawmen in Disgrace," *New Mexico Historical Review* (April 1986).

"Bandits Escape in Tradition," *New York Times* (March 11, 1934).

"Bandits, Old and New Style," *Outlook* (January 28, 1925).

"The Battle Over a Jesse James Monument," *Literary Digest* (October 29, 1927).

Bishop, Jim. "How the FBI Got John Dillinger," *Washington Evening Star* (December 5, 1962).

Blackburn, Bob. "Law Enforcement in Transition," *Chronicles of Oklahoma* (Summer 1978).

Bode, Carl, ed. *The New Mencken Letters.* New York: The Dial Press, 1977.

Boessenecker, John. *Badge and Buckshot: Lawlessness in Old California.* Norman: University of Oklahoma Press, 1988.

Bold, Christine. *Selling the Wild West: Popular Western Fiction, 1860–1960.* Bloomington: Indiana University Press, 1987.

Brant, Marley. *The Outlaw Youngers: A Confederate Brotherhood.* Lanham, Md.: Madison Books, 1992.

Breihan, Carl W. *Badmen of the Frontier Days.* New York: Robert M. McBriden Co., 1957.

———. *Lawmen and Robbers.* Caldwell, Idaho: The Caxton Printers, Ltd., 1986.

Brown, Dee. "Butch Cassidy and the Sundance Kid," *American History Illustrated* (Summer 1982).

Calhoun, Frederick S. *The Lawmen: United States Marshals and Their Deputies, 1789–1989.* New York: Penguin Books, 1991.

Campbell, Joseph. *The Power of Myth.* New York: Doubleday, 1988.

Castel, Albert. "William Clarke

Quantrill," *Civil War* (January–February 1992).

Cheatham, Gary. "Divided Loyalties in Civil War Kansas," *Kansas History* (Summer 1988).

Claitor, Diana. *Outlaws Mobsters and Murderers.* New York: M & M Books, 1991.

Cooper, Courtney Ryley. "Bandit Land," *Saturday Evening Post* (August 4, 1934).

Cordry, H. D. "Deadly Business: The Early Years of the Crime Bureau," *Chronicles of Oklahoma* (Fall 1985).

"Crime and the Movies," *Literary Digest* (May 7, 1921).

"Crime-ridden America Blushes for Its Jails," *Literary Digest* (May 5, 1934).

Dary, David. *True Tales of the Old-Time Plains.* New York: Crown Publishers, Inc., 1979.

"Dillinger Case Stirs Nation's Press to Sarcasm," *Literary Digest* (May 5, 1934).

Dugan, Mark, and Boessenecker, John. *The Grey Fox: The True Story of Bill Miner, Last of the Old-Time Bandits.* Norman: University of Oklahoma Press, 1992.

Eyewitness (Valcourt-Vermont, Edgar). *The Dalton Brothers and Their Astounding Career of Crime.* New York: Jingle Bob/Crown Publishers, Inc., 1892.

Farah, Douglas. "Shootout: Digging Up the Real Story," *Washington Post* (April 19, 1992).

Goodrich, Thomas. *Bloody Dawn: The Story of the Lawrence Massacre.* Kent, Ohio: Kent State University Press, 1991.

Hofstadter, Richard. "America As a Gun Culture," *American Heritage* (October 1970).

Horan, James D. *Desperate Men: Revelations From the Sealed Pinkerton Files.* New York: Bonanza Books, 1959.

———. *The Pinkertons: The Detective Dynasty That Made History.* New York: Bonanza Books, 1967.

"How to Fight the Forces of Crime," *Literary Digest* (January 1, 1921).

Karpis, Alvin, with Bill Trent. *The Alvin Karpis Story.* New York: Coward, McCann and Geoghegan, Inc., 1971.

Kittredge, William, and Kdrauzer, Steven. "Marshal Joe LeFors vs. Killer Tom Horn," *American West* (December 1985).

Lehman, Leola. "A Deputy U.S. Marshal in the Territories," *Chronicles of Oklahoma* (Autumn 1965).

Logan, Malcolm. "Glorifying the Criminal," *Scribner's* (July 1931).

Lomax, Alan. *The Folk Songs of North America.* New York: Doubleday and Company, 1960.

Lyon, Peter. "The Wild, Wild West," *American Heritage* (August 1960).

Marsh, Dave, and Leventhal, Harold, eds. *Pastures of Plenty: A Self- Portrait,*

Woody Guthrie. New York: Harper Collins Publishers, 1990.

McDonald, A. B. "Hamer Now Itching to Get on Trail of Dillinger," *Dallas Journal* (June 6, 1934).

McRill, Leslie. "Ingalls: The Story of a Town that Will Not Die," *Chronicles of Oklahoma* (Winter 1958–59).

Meadows, Anne. *Digging Up Butch and Sundance*. New York: St. Martins Press, 1994.

Mencken, H. L. "What to Do With Criminals," *Liberty Magazine* (July 18, 1934).

Menig, Henry. "Woody Guthrie," *Chronicles of Oklahoma* (Summer 1975).

Moley, Raymond, and Sisson, Edgar. "Crime Marches On: St. Paul—Gangster's Paradise," *Today* (June 23, 1934).

Moulton, Gary E. *The Papers of Chief John Ross*. Vol. 2. Norman: Oklahoma University Press, 1985.

Musser, Charles. *Thomas A. Edison Papers: A Guide to Motion Picture Catalogs by American Producers and Distributors, 1894–1908: A Microfilm Edition*. Frederick, Md.: University Publications of America, 1985.

Patterson, Richard. *Historical Atlas of the Outlaw West*. Boulder, Colo.: Johnson Books, 1985.

———. "Train Robbery," *American West* (March 1977).

Pinkerton, William A. *Train Robberies and Train Robbers*. Fort Davis, Tex.: Frontier Book Co., 1968.

Pointer, Larry. *In Search of Butch Cassidy*. Norman: University of Oklahoma Press, 1977.

Powers, Richard Gid. *G-Men: Hoover's FBI in American Popular Culture*. Carbondale, Ill.: Southern Illinois University Press, 1983.

———. *Secrecy and Power: The Life of J. Edgar Hoover*. New York, The Free Press, 1987.

Redford, Robert. *The Outlaw Trail: A Journey Through Time*. New York: Grosset and Dunlap, 1976.

Reedstrom, E. Lisle. "Of Mines and Men," *Wild West* (February 1994).

Rennert, Vincent. *Western Outlaws*. New York: Crowell-Collier Press, 1967.

Ridge, Martin. "The Outlaw Myth," *American History Illustrated* (Summer 1982).

"The Rising Tide of Crime," *Literary Digest* (August 15, 1925).

Robbins, Peggy. "Sam Bass: The Texas Robin Hood," *American History Illustrated* (Summer 1982).

Rosa, Joseph G. *The Gunfighter: Man or Myth?* Norman: University of Oklahoma Press, 1969.

Rosenberg, Bruce A. *The Code of the West*. Bloomington: Indiana University Press, 1982.

Settle, William A. *Jesse James Was His Name*. Lincoln: University of Nebraska Press, 1966.

Sisson, Edgar. "The Inside Story of Dillinger's Death," *Today* (August 11, 1934).

Slate, John, and Steinberg, R. U. *Lawmen Crimebusters and Champions of Justice*. New York: M & M Books, 1991.

Slotkin, Richard. *Gunfighter Nation: The Myth of the Frontier in Twentieth Century America*. New York: Harper Perennial, 1992.

Smith, Helen. "Sam Bass and the Myth Machine," *American West* (January 1970).

Smith, Robert Barr. "Shootout at Ingalls," *Wild West* (October 1992).

Steckmesser, Kent L. *The Western Hero in History and Legend*. Norman: University of Oklahoma Press, 1965.

———. "The Oklahoma Robin Hood," *American West* (January 1970).

Stolberg, Mary M. "The Evolution of Frontier Justice: The Case of Judge Isaac Parker," *Prologue* (Spring 1988).

Talley, Robert. "Capital's Famous Hoover Brothers," *Washington Post* (October 7, 1934).

Tatum, Stephen. *Inventing Billy the Kid: Visions of the Outlaw in America, 1881–1981*. Albuquerque: University of New Mexico Press, 1982.

"The Twilight of a Noble Art," *Nation* (December 26, 1923).

Toland, John. *The Dillinger Days*. New York: Random House, 1963.

Traub, Stuart. "Rewards, Bounty Hunting, and Criminal Justice in the West, 1865–1900," *Western History Quarterly* (August 1988).

Tully, Andrew. *The FBI's Most Famous Cases*. New York: William Morrow and Company, 1965.

Tuska, Jon. *The Filming of the West*. New York: Doubleday and Company, 1976.

Utley, Robert M. *Billy the Kid: A Short and Violent Life*. Lincoln: University of Nebraska Press, 1989.

Vollmer, August. "We Can Curb Crime!" *Los Angeles Times* (June 24, 1934).

Voss, Frederick, and Barber, James. *We Never Sleep: The First Fifty Years of the Pinkertons*. Washington, D.C.: Smithsonian Institution Press, 1981.

Wallis, Michael. *Pretty Boy*. New York: St. Martin's Press, 1992.

Walters, Lorenzo. *Tombstone's Yesterday*. Tucson, Ariz.: Acme Printing Company, 1928.

White, Richard. "Outlaw Gangs of the Middle Border: American Social Bandits," *Western Historical Quarterly* (October 1981).

Whitehead, Don. *The FBI Story*. New York: Random House, 1963.

Williams, Burton. "Quantrill's Raid on Lawrence," *Kansas Historical Quarterly* (Summer 1968).

Index

Italicized page numbers indicate illustrations

J

K

L

M

N

O

P